# LIFE IN CHRIST

# LIFE IN CHRIST

## A Manual for Disciples

### TONY SALERNO

with Gabriel Arosemena & Steve Harrison

**BETHANY HOUSE PUBLISHERS**
MINNEAPOLIS, MINNESOTA 55438
A Division of Bethany Fellowship, Inc.

ISBN 0–87123–887–X

Copyright © 1983 Agape Force
All Rights Reserved

First Printing, May 1983—10,000
Second Printing, March 1984—5,000
Third Printing, February 1985—10,000
Fourth Printing, January 1986—10,000
Fifth Printing, October 1986—4,000
Sixth Printing, January 1987—5,000
Seventh Printing, February 1988—4,000

Published by Bethany House Publishers
A Division of Bethany Fellowship, Inc.
6820 Auto Club Road, Minneapolis, MN 55438

Printed in the United States of America

**Art Direction: Tony Salerno**
**Design: Cynthia Kuiper**
**Graphics: Cynthia Hilliard**

*Life in Christ: A Manual for Discipleship*, is illustrated with the art of Gustave Dore (1832–1883). Many of these etchings were originally created for *The Holy Bible, with Illustrations by Gustave Dore*, published in 1866, and are reproduced by permission.

# Foreword

*Life in Christ: A Manual for Discipleship* is one of the most important study guides ever published. It is doctrinally correct, comprehensive and easy to understand. I recommend it to all seekers of truth, including new converts, established believers, and even ministers.

Too much of what is written today for new converts is shallow and incomplete. It often lacks spiritual authority and depth. Not so with *Life in Christ: A Manual for Discipleship*. Within these pages you will discover what it really means to be a true believer. You will learn about the loving terms of discipleship such as obedience, restitution, absolute surrender and service to mankind. You will also learn who God is, how deeply He loves, and how He responds to all we experience. There are important lessons on prayer, Bible study, the Holy Spirit, temptation, and fellowship with other believers; also, how to share your faith.

Please do not skim through this material. Your spiritual growth is at stake. Read one chapter at a time and pray that the Holy Spirit will give you understanding of all you read. Satan can never rob you of truth that is fully understood. Obey the Word as it comes to you. For example, when reading about restitution—do it! Prayer—do it! Forgiveness—do it!

This could be one of the most important books you have ever studied. It is not an accident it was placed in your hands. Evidently, the Spirit of God is leading you into a new stage of growth and spiritual power.

Thank you, Tony Salerno—and all your Agape Force staff—for giving us such an honest, soul-searching guide.

As a result of this study guide, thousands of new converts as well as established believers will move from the shallow waters of half-heartedness into the deep waters of God's fullness.

It is with great joy in the Lord that I recommend *Life in Christ: A Manual for Discipleship* to you! Here is truth that can set you free.

In Christ's love,
David Wilkerson

# PREFACE

Since you have exercised repentance toward God and faith toward our Lord and Savior Jesus Christ, you are now in the family of the Living God. As a new brother or sister in the precious faith, you are welcomed as a fellow traveler to the city of God.

This book in no way pretends to be a substitute for reading the Bible, but it is intended to give pointers to help you in your untried faith and new walk with God.

Any great preacher or well-known saint whom you have admired was once a "babe in Christ." The same resources that produced such spiritual maturity are open to you. You have an open heaven through the Christ who constantly intercedes for you. You have an open Bible, a book just packed with intelligent encouragement. You have the fellowship of the believers.

Our prayers will follow you daily.   Leonard Ravenhill

TONY SALERNO is the president and founder of Agape Force, an evangelism outreach which has sent ministry teams throughout the U.S. and overseas. They have developed and produced many record albums, children's books, videos and films. Salerno, principle author of LIFE IN CHRIST, developed the manual to help new Christians advance past conversion to a deeply committed Christian lifestyle.

STEVE HARRISON was converted to Christ through the ministry of Agape Force and is now a full-time staff member. As well as co-writing LIFE IN CHRIST, he has been responsible for leading ministry teams and coordinating major evangelism outreaches in the U.S. and Canada. He is a member of the Agape Force Executive Committee.

GABRIEL AROSEMENA joined the Agape Force in 1976. His involvement began in the music division with the groups Candle and Sweetwater and the musical "Agapeland." He has directed the Agape Force Discipleship Training Institute in Oklahoma. He is currently involved with Ridgecrest, an extension of the Agape Force dedicated to training Christian artists and musicians.

# TABLE OF CONTENTS

Introduction........ix
Instructions for the Proper Use of This Manual...xiii

**My New Life in Christ • 1**

**Community of Believers • 35**

**Sword of the Spirit • 55**

**Life-Breath of the Soul • 83**

**Knowledge of the Holy One • 109**

**Heart of God • 139**

**Badge of Love • 165**

**Testing of Your Faith • 187**

**Sharing My New Life • 211**

**Power from God • 239**

**Registry • 261**

© Copyright 1983 by Agape Force

# INTRODUCTION

id you know the Bible says the angels of God rejoice when even one sinner repents? It's a great occasion in heaven. And, like the father of the prodigal son, God rejoices over the return of each of His lost children. As you give your heart to Christ, you will begin to share in His love and bring great joy to the heart of God.

Often, those—like you—who want to open their hearts to Jesus do so at a large gathering—a church, Christian concert, or visiting evangelist's crusade. You may be asked to surrender your life to Christ and given instructions on how to meet Him. However, you may still need more explanation or have some questions of what to do next. Similarly, when a friend of yours or even a stranger witnesses to you, you may give your life to Christ without knowing what the next step should be. Because so many of those who first come to Jesus have a limited concept of what following Him is all about, the purpose of this handbook is to fill the gap and firmly establish the new walk with Christ.

### True Conversion

At a tent revival in the Midwest a young man made a superficial commitment to Christ, not really understanding what was involved. Because of this, he still partied and drank with the gang, prayed only when something went wrong in his life and never seemed to have time for Bible reading. Periodic bouts of remorse drew him to church or to evangelistic crusades, but not much changed. After five years of marriage, his wife discovered he was being unfaithful and left to live with her parents. At the age of 37, broke, alone, jobless, friendless, he got down on his knees before God, wept and prayed for forgiveness and a new start. God heard him. "My life finally changed," said the young man. "I realized I had never given up the things of the world before. I was lying to God in my heart, and was crucifying Jesus all over again. It took me twenty years to find out what a real commitment to Christ was, that Jesus was real and alive, that He cares how I live.

Nothing grieves the Heavenly Father more than to see one of His precious lost ones receive Christ's forgiveness only to go on living as if nothing had really happened. We are called to salvation as a preparation for an ongoing relationship with Christ under His Lordship. That's what it means to make Jesus your Savior and Lord. God has a purpose and a job for you—more exciting, fulfilling and challenging than anything you can possibly imagine. He may lead you to be a bricklayer, secretary, scientist, or something else, but these will now serve as avenues to fulfill an even greater purpose; that is to be a testimony of God's love and faithfulness anywhere in the world.

The lessons in this handbook should be done with prayerful reverence toward God. Do them thoughtfully, with the kind of care you would expect to spend on a single most important event in your life. Getting started right will prevent many hindrances and sorrows from coming up later, hindrances that often suddenly erupt in the lives of those who enter too casually, too thoughtlessly, too carelessly, into life with the King of kings and Lord of lords.

Jesus offers us unconditional love, and it is a healing, uplifting, life-changing love, for those who open their hearts to receive it. Sometimes new believers fail to understand that you have to give your "whole life" to Christ to get a new "whole life" back from Him. You can't smuggle "just a little sin" or "just a little piece of the world" into His kingdom. Those who try will often wonder why their hearts remain hungry, restless, depressed, unsatisfied, stale, bored or hurting. Let Jesus have it all.

The Bible says you can't put new wine into old, stiff wineskins or they will burst. You can't bring the old astrology or magic games into your new life. You can't bring in bitterness toward your father or unforgiveness toward an old friend. You can't bring drugs or drunkenness. You can't hold onto pride, sarcasm, gossip, rebellion or resentment. Sexual relationships outside marriage are out. All these things are cheap worldly counterfeits of the precious gift the Heavenly Father has for you!

**Seven Names**

Seven names given to followers of Christ in the Scriptures: saints, for their holiness; believers, for their faith; brethren, for their love; disciples, for their knowledge; soldiers, for their discipline; witnesses, for their life's work; Christians, for their Christlike example. —Selected

"Hitherto have ye asked nothing in my name," Jesus said, "ask, and ye shall receive, that your joy may be full."

To reach out and receive what Jesus has promised, you have to put down what is in your hands right now. Empty your hands and heart, lift them up to Jesus, and expect your joy to "be made full."

Keep in mind that the Bible doesn't always promise us an easy way. Christian life has trials, temptations, suffering and persecutions, as is to be expected in life. You may lose friends or get fired from jobs because of your beliefs, and there may be times when you feel God has forgotten you. King David felt that way at times, even though the Bible calls him a man after God's own heart. But God never forgot David, nor will he forget you. God will never put you in a situation which His grace and power can't bring you through, and there is always great rejoicing when you realize how God has strengthened you or taught you a valuable lesson through a tough situation. "They that sow in tears shall reap in joy," we are told in Psalm 126:5.

# Instructions for the Proper Use of This Manual

**This textbook is designed to provide a brief outline in the study of basic principles essential to a Christian. It is hoped that the value of discipline and consistency in its study will help to afterwards yield "the peaceable fruit of righteousness" (Hebrews 12:11). The following counsel is offered to those who use it:**

1. Set aside a special time each day for its examination. If at all possible, find a quiet place where you can be alone with God.

2. Sincerely invite God the Holy Spirit to be an active participant in your study. Remember that, "... when he, the Spirit of truth, is come, he will guide you into all truth ..."(John 16:13); and also, "But the Comforter, which is the Holy Ghost, whom the Father will send in my name, he shall teach you all things, and bring all things to your remembrance, whatsoever I have said unto you"(John 14:26). Stand firm upon these promises. *Expect* the Spirit's help!

3. After you have found the proper atmosphere and have invited God to help you, read the lessons carefully and thoughtfully.

4. When you have finished a lesson, go through it again. With all your heart and on your knees before God, review it part by part. Be careful not to leave one part for the next until it is clearly understood, heartily accepted, and solemnly decided upon.

5. After you have completed this manual, it would be beneficial to review it from time to time, remembering these important beginning and foundational principles.

6. Important: It would be advisable and most beneficial to get someone (i.e. an older or more mature Christian) to review each chapter after you have completed it. For the sake of identification, we will call this assistant your *helper*.

7. The Scripture references used in this manual are taken from the *King James Version* unless otherwise indicated.

### Cabbage Head?

You can go through this textbook in a hurry but it would be far more beneficial and lasting to take your time, digest the content, and practically apply it to your everyday life.

There was once a young man who was exceptionally bright. When he was ready, his father went to enroll him in a fine university and said to the President of that school, "Since my son is so gifted, would it be possible for him to finish the courses in less than the normal time?"

"It all depends on what you want your son to be," the wise president replied. "If you want him to be a great oak, it will take awhile. But if you want him to be a cabbage, I can have him ready in no time."

Chapter One

# My New Life in Christ

## Section One

**"For God so loved the world, that he gave his only begotten Son, that whosoever believeth in him should not perish, but have everlasting life." (John 3:16)**

It is God's plan to restore you to the restful, holy and happy relationship with Him that He intended when He made you. How can you know this is true? The Bible says, "For this is good and acceptable in the sight of God our Savior; who will have all men to be saved, and to come unto the knowledge of the truth" (1 Timothy 2:3-4). God's plan is called salvation.

Jesus died as a substitute for the penalty of our sins, shedding His blood for you and me, so we could be saved. Jesus said, "I am the door: by me if any man enter in, he shall be saved . . ." (John 10:9). To receive new life in Christ, we must die to our old selfish ways and accept cleansing through His forgiveness.

Many who come to Christ take their past sins too lightly, perhaps feeling they have led "good" lives. Others feel they have done such terrible things that God can never fully accept them. Jesus, Himself, said, "there is none good but one, that is, God" (Mark 10:18); and Isaiah 53:6 tells us, "All we like sheep have gone astray." It is almost humanly impossible to understand how even the "smallest" sins have grieved God, or how even the greatest sins are washed completely clean in His loving forgiveness. Let's not take sin lightly on the one hand, nor underestimate our Lord's capacity for forgiveness on the other hand.

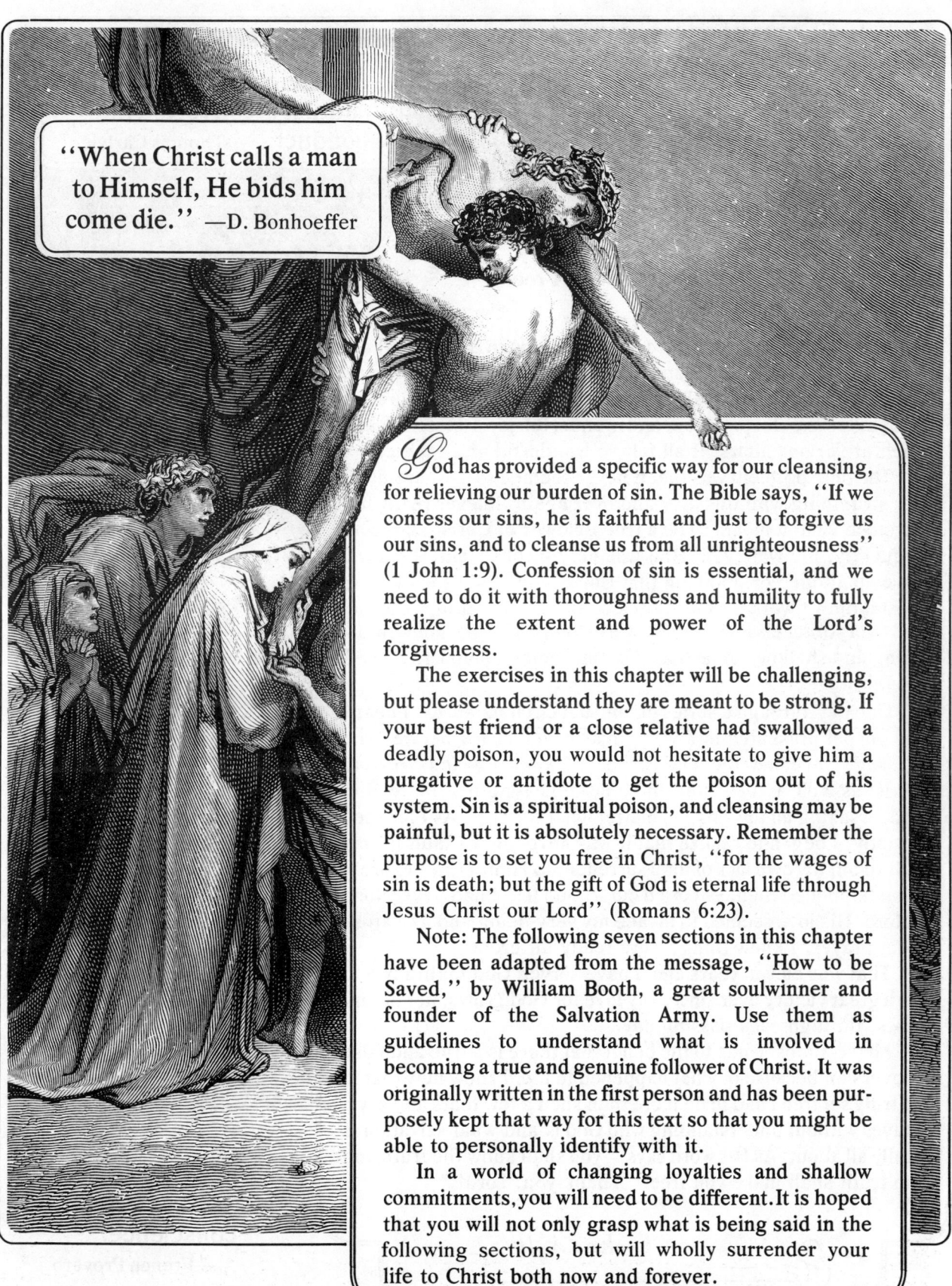

"When Christ calls a man to Himself, He bids him come die." —D. Bonhoeffer

God has provided a specific way for our cleansing, for relieving our burden of sin. The Bible says, "If we confess our sins, he is faithful and just to forgive us our sins, and to cleanse us from all unrighteousness" (1 John 1:9). Confession of sin is essential, and we need to do it with thoroughness and humility to fully realize the extent and power of the Lord's forgiveness.

The exercises in this chapter will be challenging, but please understand they are meant to be strong. If your best friend or a close relative had swallowed a deadly poison, you would not hesitate to give him a purgative or antidote to get the poison out of his system. Sin is a spiritual poison, and cleansing may be painful, but it is absolutely necessary. Remember the purpose is to set you free in Christ, "for the wages of sin is death; but the gift of God is eternal life through Jesus Christ our Lord" (Romans 6:23).

Note: The following seven sections in this chapter have been adapted from the message, "How to be Saved," by William Booth, a great soulwinner and founder of the Salvation Army. Use them as guidelines to understand what is involved in becoming a true and genuine follower of Christ. It was originally written in the first person and has been purposely kept that way for this text so that you might be able to personally identify with it.

In a world of changing loyalties and shallow commitments, you will need to be different. It is hoped that you will not only grasp what is being said in the following sections, but will wholly surrender your life to Christ both now and forever.

"Conviction is worthless until it is converted into conduct."—Thomas Carlyle

### The Truth Set Me Free

In the past, I've responded to convictions in my heart that I knew were from God. Evangelistic services, church retreats, and Christian concerts all affected me to a certain degree. I remember the deep sorrow and wonderful joy I received as I knelt at various altars. It all felt so wonderful and exciting.

The only problem was that it never seemed to last. I remember struggling with this over and over again. I never really understood what it meant to be a true follower of Christ and, consequently, my walk with Him was very inconsistent. Finally I gave up altogether, thinking that Christianity didn't work or at least it didn't work for me. I became involved in drugs, alcohol and everything else my friends were doing. This seemed unfulfilling and shallow, but at least I wasn't being a hypocrite—so I thought.

One day, through a series of unusual circumstances, I heard the gospel presented in a way I had never heard before. The message revealed the importance of *knowing* and *trusting* Christ as well as believing in Him, dedicating my life to Him and forsaking all my sins, no matter what the cost. As I listened intently, I began to realize that it was never God's fault for my failure but my own lack of total surrender to Him. I can't express what happened then, as I cried out to God like I had never done before. His love seemed to invade my very being and as I arose from prayer, I knew things were really different.

That was eleven years ago. I have served God faithfully and with great victory ever since. My love for God grows, not diminishes, through each passing day.

I have almost come to the belief that there is a true and false conversion because of what happened to me. I know now that to be truly set free I had to do more than shed a few tears and say a prayer without understanding who God is and what salvation is really all about. As His word says, "you shall know the truth and the truth shall make you free." Thank you, Lord!

*Richard H.*

"There is no pillow so soft as a clear conscience."
—French Proverb

# Realization of Sin

*I* freely admit that I am a sinner. I've sinned against my God, against my neighbors and against my own soul. I've sinned in the world, in my business and pleasures. I've done many things I should not have done and left undone things I should have done.

I will not cover my sins. They are more than I can count and grievous beyond the possibility of calculation. They have dishonored my Heavenly Father; treated the sacrifice of Jesus with contempt; exercised a bad influence upon the members of my own family as well as upon those who have known me in the world. I deserve the everlasting displeasure of God, and I see that if I die in my sins, I shall fall into the damnation of Hell.

O Lord, have mercy upon me!

Psalm 51:4; Isaiah 53:6
   Whom have I sinned against?

Romans 3:23
   Who has sinned against God?

Romans 6:23
   What is the result of my sin?

Psalm 14:3
   What have I and all other sinners done?

6

# Sorrow for Sin

*Not* only do I see that I've sinned against God, but I am truly sorry for what I've done. I honestly hate my evil ways, and I deeply regret the damage that has been done for having followed them. I am grieved on account of my sins—not only because they have led me to the brink of Hell, but because they have been committed against my Heavenly Father who has continually loved and cared for me.

If I could undo the past, I'd gladly do so; but I can't! The sins I've committed are written down against me in the book of God's remembrance. No prayers I can offer, no tears I can shed, no mourning I can do, nor good works I can perform will remove that terrible record. My only hope is in the forgiving mercy of Jesus Christ who has said, "Him that cometh to Me I will in no wise cast out."

Psalm 38:17-18
   What should my sin lead me to do?

_____

2 Corinthians 7:9
   What should my sorrow lead me to do?

_____

Psalm 32:3-5
   What are some results of sin which appeared in David's life (and could also appear in mine)?

_____
_____

1 Kings 8:37-40
   The people of Israel were given instructions for dealing with their sin. How can I follow this pattern?

_____
_____
_____

# Confession of Sin

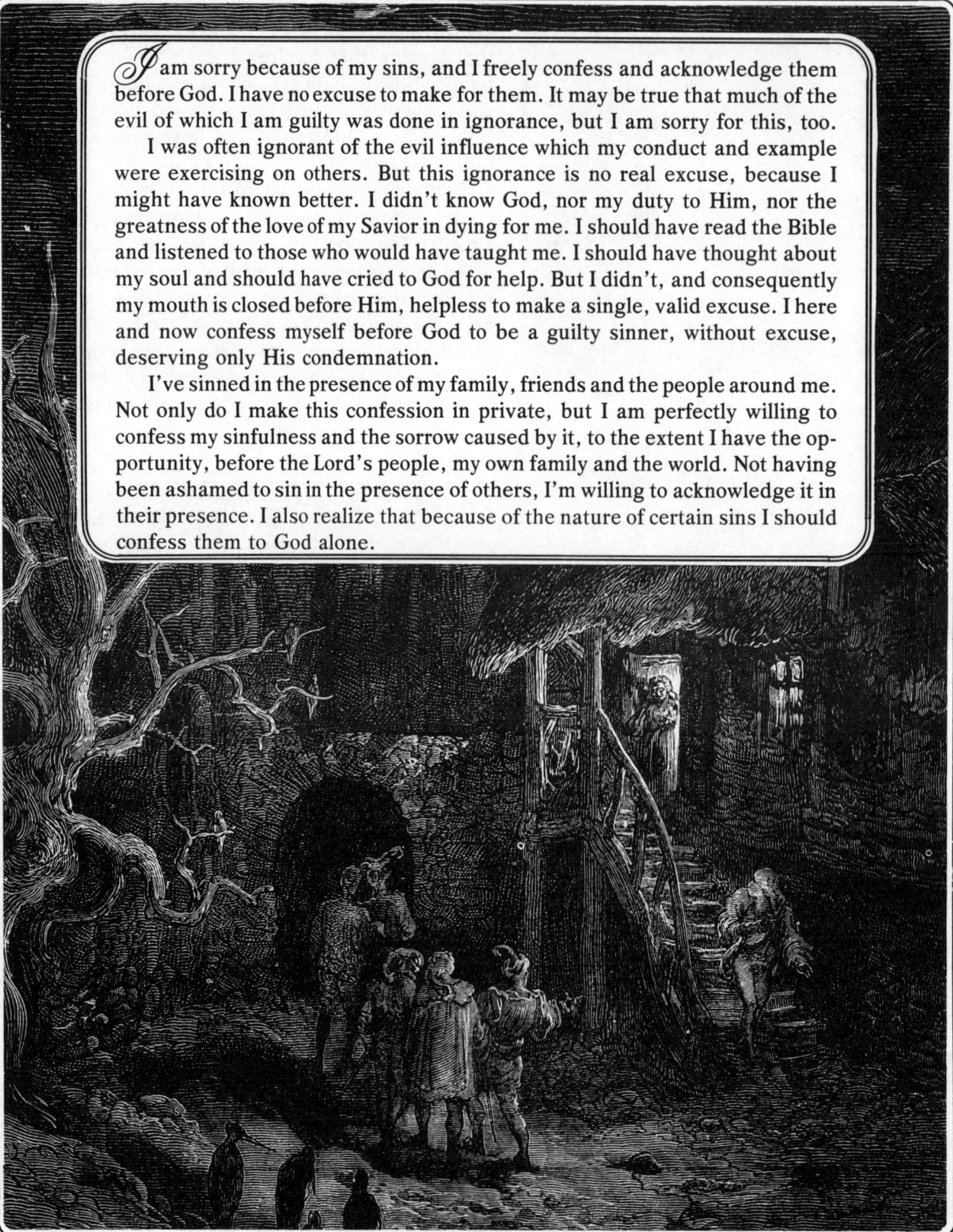

I am sorry because of my sins, and I freely confess and acknowledge them before God. I have no excuse to make for them. It may be true that much of the evil of which I am guilty was done in ignorance, but I am sorry for this, too.

I was often ignorant of the evil influence which my conduct and example were exercising on others. But this ignorance is no real excuse, because I might have known better. I didn't know God, nor my duty to Him, nor the greatness of the love of my Savior in dying for me. I should have read the Bible and listened to those who would have taught me. I should have thought about my soul and should have cried to God for help. But I didn't, and consequently my mouth is closed before Him, helpless to make a single, valid excuse. I here and now confess myself before God to be a guilty sinner, without excuse, deserving only His condemnation.

I've sinned in the presence of my family, friends and the people around me. Not only do I make this confession in private, but I am perfectly willing to confess my sinfulness and the sorrow caused by it, to the extent I have the opportunity, before the Lord's people, my own family and the world. Not having been ashamed to sin in the presence of others, I'm willing to acknowledge it in their presence. I also realize that because of the nature of certain sins I should confess them to God alone.

Psalm 32:5
  To whom should I confess my sin?

___

Daniel 9:3-5
  How will I follow Daniel's example?

___

James 5:16
  To whom else should I confess?

___

1 John 1:9
  What is the result of confessing my sin?

___

# Turning Away From Sin

*I have seen myself to be a sinner and have confessed my sins before God and others. With God's help I now renounce and turn away from every one of my past sins. Whatever pleasure sin may have brought me in the past and whatever earthly gain temptation may promise me in the future, I here and now, in the strength of God, put sin away from my life, never to go back again.*

**Psalm 24:3-4**
What kind of people is God looking for?

_____

**Psalm 34:13-14**
What do these instructions mean to me?

_____
_____

**Psalm 119:9-11**
(Rewritten in my own words)

_____
_____
_____
_____

**Proverbs 28:13**
What happens to the people who turn from their sin?

_____

**Ezekiel 18:31**
What is the instruction for me here concerning my sin?

_____

**Isaiah 1:16**
What does the prophet Isaiah say about turning from sin?

_____

_____

### Tied To The World

There were once two men who, under the influence of liquor, came down one night to where their boat was tied. They wanted to return home, so they got in and began to row. They pulled away hard all night, wondering why they never got to the other side of the bay. When the gray dawn of morning broke, to their amazement, they had never untied the boat from the dock or raised the anchor. And that's just the way it is with many who are striving to enter the kingdom of heaven. They cannot believe, because they are tied to this world.

# Asking Forgiveness for Sin

*Feeling how shamefully I've rebelled against my Heavenly Father (in despising His love, in breaking His commandments and influencing others to do the same), I submit myself to Him here on my knees right now. Lord, I humbly pray that you will have mercy upon me, a miserable sinner; and I ask you for Christ's sake to forgive all my sins, to receive me into your arms; and to make me, unworthy though I am, a member of your family.*

**Daniel 9:19**
  Following Daniel's example, what should be my plea to God?

_____
_____
_____

**Matthew 6:9-13**
  What does the Lord's Prayer say about forgiveness?

_____
_____
_____
_____

**Luke 18:10-14**
  What was the difference between the Pharisee and the tax collector in their prayers to God?

_____
_____
_____

# Commitment

> *I promise you, Heavenly Father, in your strength and with all my heart as you forgive me and receive me into your favor, that I determine from now on to be your faithful servant, spending the rest of my days doing what I can for your glory, for the extension of your kingdom and for the salvation of those around me.*

Psalm 37:5
 What does this verse say about commitment?

_____

_____

Romans 12:1-2
 What are some things I should practice as a Christian?

_____

_____

_____

_____

# Faith

*I* believe that Jesus Christ, God's Son, in His great mercy and love, having died for me in my place, bore my sins in His own body on the cross.

Believing this, I here and now welcome you, Jesus, to my heart as my Savior from hell, from sin, from the power of the devil and from my own self-righteousness.

Your Word says that if I come to you, you will in no wise cast me out; and I come to you with all my heart just now, as a helpless, guilty sinner, seeking salvation and trusting only in your blood.

I am sure you will not reject me. Rather, I believe at this very moment you are taking me into your family. Thank you for forgiving me and for your precious blood that washes all my sins away. You were wounded for my transgressions; you were bruised for my iniquities; the punishment I should have received was laid upon you; and by your sufferings I am healed.

I am forgiven! Praise the Lord! Thank you, Jesus, for salvation!

Psalm 121:1-8
List some of the ways God displays His care.

Proverbs 30:5
Why can I trust in God's Word?

Jeremiah 17:7-8
When I trust in the Lord, what is the result?

Isaiah 7:9
When I don't trust in the Lord, what is the result?

Hebrews 11:6
How does this verse apply to me personally?

Hebrews 10:38
How shall I live my new life in Christ?

# ~ Personal Prayer ~

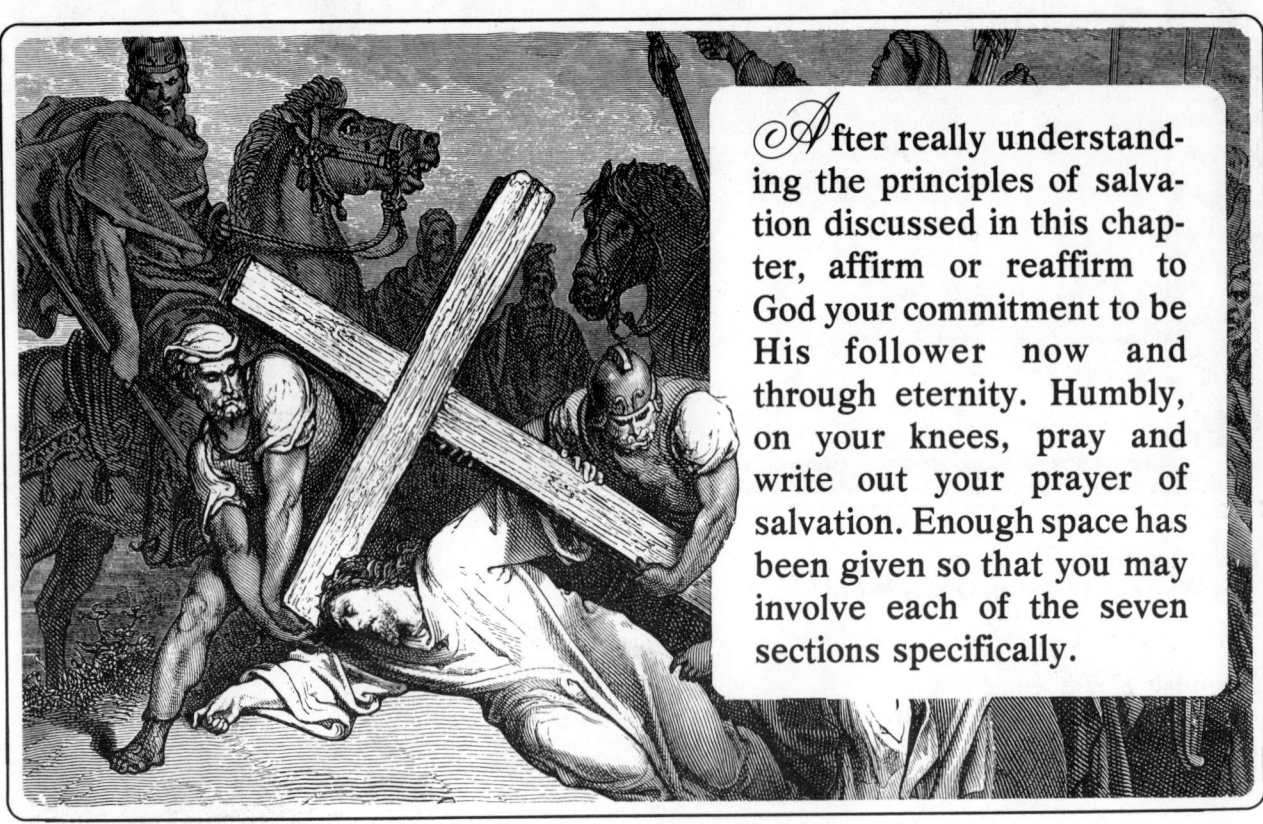

*After* really understanding the principles of salvation discussed in this chapter, affirm or reaffirm to God your commitment to be His follower now and through eternity. Humbly, on your knees, pray and write out your prayer of salvation. Enough space has been given so that you may involve each of the seven sections specifically.

### Realization of Sin

*Dear Heavenly Father...*

### Sorrow for Sin

### Confession of Sin

## Turning Away From Sin

## Asking Forgiveness for Sin

## Commitment

## Faith

*You will now want to fill out the Birth Certificate.* See REGISTRY

## Prayer of Thanks

## Section Two

# Forgiveness

The Lord's Prayer instructs us to forgive others as God has forgiven us. If we don't forgive others, our Heavenly Father will not forgive us.

You will want to ask your father and mother forgiveness for any sins you may have committed against them. If they have hurt you either willfully or unintentionally, forgive them, recognizing that the fifth commandment says, "Honor thy father and thy mother: that thy days may be long upon the land which the Lord thy God giveth thee" (Exodus 20:12).

Secondly, you will want to ask others of your family (brothers, sisters, your husband or wife, children, other relatives, etc.) forgiveness for any sins you may have committed against them. If any of these have hurt you either willfully or unintentionally, forgive them, recognizing Jesus' command to forgive others "Until seventy times seven" (Matthew 18:22).

Thirdly, you will want to do the same with all your friends, teachers, persons in authority (policemen, government officials, employers, etc.).

Lastly, you will want to forgive anyone who may have wronged you and ask the Lord to show you how to love them. In turn, ask forgiveness of any of these or others you have sinned against.

I praise and glorify you, Lord, for forgiving me and for helping me forgive those who have sinned against me. I pray now that you would cleanse my heart from any root of bitterness, hate or anger. I want to love as you loved and forgive as you have forgiven me.

Matthew 5:23-24
What should I do before I come to the Lord with my offering?

_____

_____

Matthew 5:43-44
How should I respond to enemies and persecutors?

_____

_____

Matthew 18:21-22
   a) How many times should I forgive a person who sins against me?
   _____

   b) What do you think Jesus meant by this statement?
   _____
   _____


Matthew 18:23-35
   What is the point of this story?
   _____
   _____
   _____

Mark 11:25
   What should I do before I pray?
   _____
   _____
   _____


Matthew 6:14-15
   What is one condition of receiving forgiveness from God?
   _____
   _____
   _____

**Grandfather's Apology**

*N*ever be ashamed to apologize when you have done wrong to someone in your family. Let that be a law in your home. The best thing I ever heard about my grandfather, whom I never saw, was this: having rebuked one of his children and having found later that he had been misinformed concerning the child's actions, he gathered all his family together in the evening of the same day, and said: "Now, I have one explanation to make and one thing to say. Thomas, this morning I rebuked you very unfairly. I am very sorry for it. I rebuked you in the presence of the whole family, and now I ask your forgiveness in their presence." It must have taken some courage to do that.—Talmage

# Restitution

$\mathscr{S}$alvation consists of restoring a person to a proper and happy relationship with God. As this relationship deepens, it becomes natural to want to reconcile those things which have hurt God and His creation. Where there was once unbelief, there is now trust. Where there was once anger and irreverence towards God, there is now love and respect.

Unfortunately, many people besides God are also hurt when we do not live in accordance with His laws. It may have been an immoral relationship, an item stolen from a store owner, a slanderous lie spoken against someone we disliked. Whatever it was, one thing is certain: others were hurt wrongfully by our sin.

Just as a convicted robber would show his sincerity and intent to be a law abiding citizen by confessing his wrong and restoring the stolen goods to their proper owner, so it is with our relationship with the Judge of all the Universe. If we are truly sorry for our sin and have promised God that we will live according to His wise laws, then we will want to confess and pay back those we have wronged. It is the only way to conquer injustice and get revenge on sin.

We must remember that restitution or "restoring back" should be made only as to the extent of our sin. If we've sinned against an individual, then we should confess it to that person alone. If we've sinned against a group, then our confession should be to the group. In this way we will begin to effectively oppose the disintegration of our society by reversing the effects of sin and showing the world what a Christian stands for.

Proverbs 28:13
   a) What is a condition for prosperity?

   b) What are conditions for receiving mercy from God?

Numbers 5:5-7
Explain the law of restitution found in the Old Testament.

Luke 19:8
   a) What did Zacchaeus declare to Christ?

   b) What did this show about Zacchaeus' heart?

---

**S. S. Teacher 'Fesses Up**

A man went to a friend of mine and said: "I don't know what is wrong with me. I teach a Sunday School class of young men, and I have tried to bring them to Jesus, and I have failed. Can you tell me why?"

"Yes," was the answer. "There's something wrong with you. You've done something wrong."

The man hesitated, but finally he said, "You're right. Years ago I was cashier in a business house, and one time the books balanced and there was some money left over. I took that money and I have kept it. That was twelve years ago. Here is the money in this envelope."

"Take it back to the owner," said my friend. "It's not yours, and it's not mine."

"But I can't do that," said the man. "I am making a salary of $22,000 a year now, and I have a wife and daughters, and my firm will never employ a dishonest man."

"Well, that's your business," said my friend. "I have advised you, and that's all I can do; but God will never forgive you until you've given that money back."

The man sank into a chair and covered his eyes for a while. Then he got up and said, "I'll do it." He took a Chesapeake and Ohio train and went to Philadelphia, and went to a great merchant prince in whose employ he had been, and told his story. The merchant prince shut and locked the door. "Let us pray," he said. They knelt together, the great merchant's arm about his visitor; and when they got up the great merchant said: "Go in peace. God bless you."

On the next Sunday the man who had confessed took the Bible on his knee as he sat before his class, and said to them: "Young men, I often wondered why I couldn't win any of you to Christ. My life was wrong, and I've repented and made it right." That man won his entire class for Christ, and they joined Dr. McKibben's church at Walnut Hills, Cincinnati, Ohio.

If you would get right with God what would be the result? Why, you would save your city.—Billy Sunday

## ~≋ Exercise ≋~

Dear Lord,
I know you want me to forgive as you forgive and have right relationships with family, relatives, friends, or enemies. Remind me now of those people with whom I need to make things right.

_____
_____
_____
_____
_____
_____
_____
_____
_____
_____

Dear Lord,
I know you want me to make things right that I have wronged (i.e. stolen articles, debts, lies, dishonesty, etc.). Please remind me now of things that I must take care of.

_____
_____
_____
_____
_____
_____
_____
_____
_____
_____

## Section Three
# Special Areas

*If* you have been involved in occult practices or false religions (or both), go through the following exercises. Even if you have not, it is suggested that you review the following two sections. This will help you to better understand how to help others who are involved in these spiritual counterfeits.

# Occult Practices

*In* our time, interest in occult practices, non-Christian meditation, games or groups has escalated sharply. Even people who call themselves Christians have claimed that such gifts as clairvoyance, telepathy, astral travel, divination, spiritism and other forms of psychic and occult abilities are "gifts from God." Many others have innocently played such games as Dungeons and Dragons, or toyed with the Ouija board, astrology and tarot cards, or tried to develop ESP (extra-sensory perception). Transcendental Meditation (TM) and other such practices are basically occult in nature. We have also seen witchcraft and Satan worship come into the open in our time.

All occult phenomena belong to the kingdom of darkness, no matter how harmless they may seem. Let's see what the Bible says about them.

Deuteronomy 18:10-12
   How does the Lord view occult practices like divination, witchcraft, reading omens, sorcery, casting spells, psychic mediums, spiritism and calling up the dead?

_____

_____

_____

Leviticus 19:26,31; 20:6
   What do these verses say about divination (revealing secret knowledge), soothsaying (foretelling the future), mediums and spiritists?
   _____
   _____

1 Chronicles 10:13
   What two reasons does this verse give for Saul's death?
   _____
   _____

2 Kings 21:6
   What was God's response to Manasseh's involvement with the occult?
   _____

Zechariah 10:2
   a) What does the prophet say of the teraphim (idols used for fortunetelling) and diviners?
   _____
   _____
   _____

   b) What happened to the people who listened to them?
   _____
   _____
   _____

Acts 16:16-18
   How did Paul respond to the girl with the spirit of divination?
   _____
   _____
   _____

Acts 19:19
   When those practicing occult arts in Ephesus heard Paul preach, what did they do with their books?
   _____

Galatians 5:19-21
   Notice that idolatry and sorcery are included among the "deeds of the flesh." What will happen to those who practice them?

Deuteronomy 29:29
   a) To whom do the "secret things" belong?

   b) To whom do the "revealed things" (prophesies, Scriptures) belong?

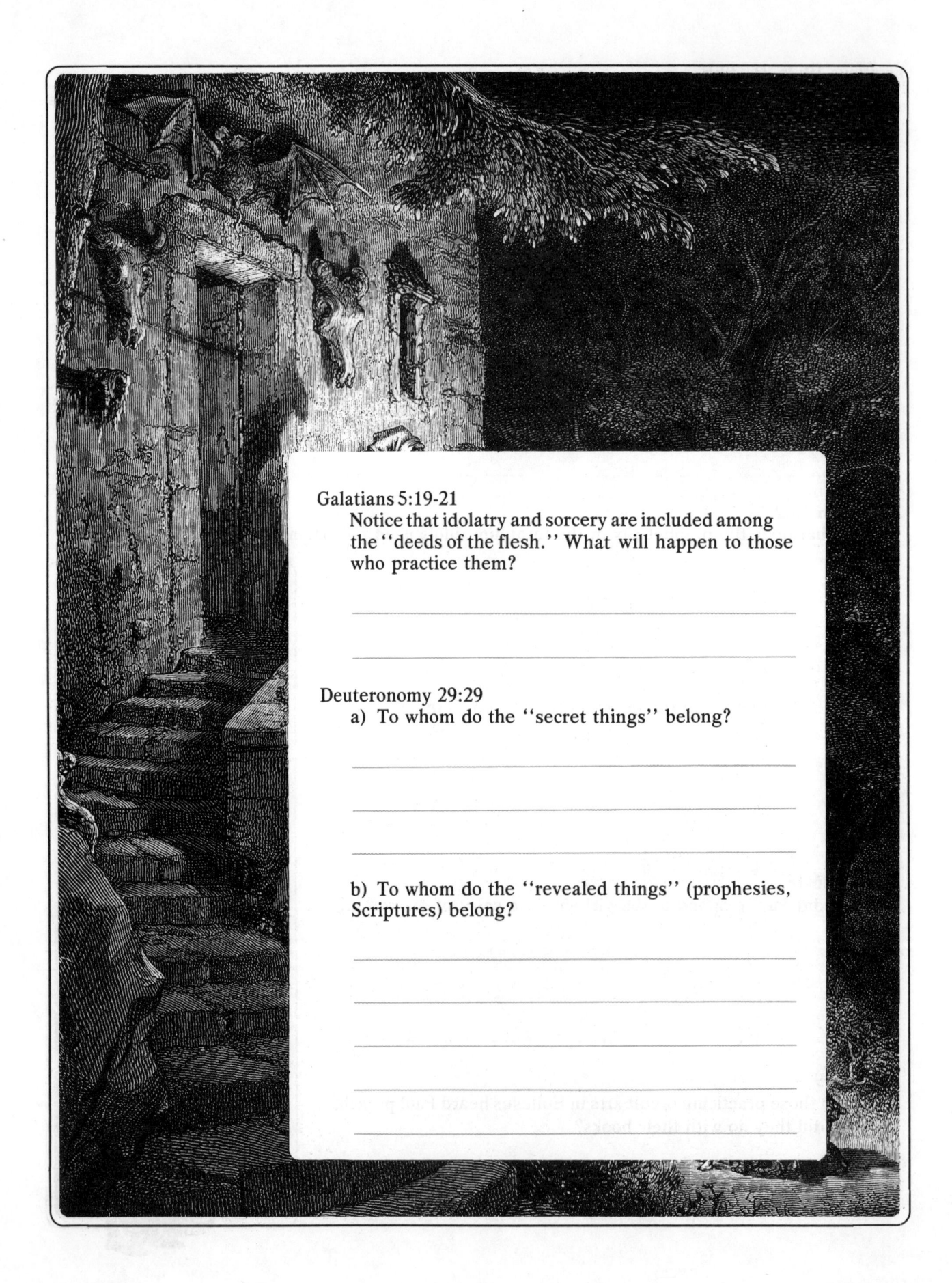

# Prayer

*L*ord Jesus, I realize that all supernatural occurrences must come from God or Satan, and all occult practices are from Satan and are an abomination to God. I confess my involvement with occult practices and I turn away from them, asking your forgiveness.

I ask that anything I have forgotten and anything my ancestors have done be included in this prayer, and I pray that the chain of consequences to my children, children's children and further generations be broken in the name of Jesus.

I now ask you, Jesus, to rebuke the demonic spirits, through your blood and in your name, commanding them to leave the same way they came in, through the occult door, and close that door forever.

Heavenly Father, I thank and praise you for your Son Jesus, in whom I have salvation. I ask the Holy Spirit to fill all the places in my spirit, soul and body formerly occupied by any beings of darkness.

# False Religions and Cults

Eastern and western religions that deny the deity of Christ, or the Biblical view that Jesus is God, are false religions and are condemned under the First Commandment.

"Thou shalt have no other gods before me. Thou shalt not make unto thee any graven image, or any likeness of any thing that is in heaven above, or that is in the earth beneath, or that is in the water under the earth: Thou shalt not bow down thyself to them, nor serve them: for I the Lord thy God am a jealous God, visiting the iniquities of the fathers upon the children unto the third and fourth generation of them that hate me" (Exodus 20:3-5).

Jesus said, "I am the way, the truth, and the life: no man cometh unto the Father, but by me" (John 14:6). There is no way to worship and follow God except through Jesus. All religions which deny or alter the Biblical view of Jesus, or preach any gospel other than the Bible teaches, are false and are under the dominion of Satan.

If you have served or now serve a religion you believe may be false, do the following exercises and pray the prayer at the end of them.

> The distinction between Christianity and all other systems of religion consists largely in this, that in these others, men are found seeking after God, while Christianity is God seeking after man.—Thomas Arnold

1 Kings 11:4-11
What happened to Solomon when he worshipped false gods?

Deuteronomy 29:24-28
How will God respond if His people serve other gods?

28

1 Kings 18:17-40
   What is the lesson Elijah wanted the people of Israel to learn?

1 Timothy 6:3-4
   What are signs of a false religion?

2 Timothy 4:3,4
   What are some things that can hinder people from the truth of Christ?

Matthew 24:5,11,24
   What are some things Jesus said would happen at "the end of the age?"

## Prayer

Heavenly Father, I confess before you on my knees, with the deepest humility and sorrow, that I have served a false god in violation of your commandment. I praise and thank you for removing the blindness from my eyes, and in the name of Jesus, I ask your forgiveness. I turn from my sin and cast myself on your mercy, praying that you will not visit my iniquity on my children, my children's children, or any further generations of my family.

I renounce Satan, his kingdom, and the demonic power behind the god and the religion (name it) I once served, in the name of Jesus, for Scripture says: "You shall have no other gods before Me."

I confess Jesus as my Lord and Savior, and Him only will I serve. I ask the Holy Spirit to fill all places in my spirit, soul and body formerly occupied by other spirits. Thank you, Heavenly Father, for the shed blood of your Son Jesus, which saves and protects me from all the powers of darkness. Amen.

## Section Four
# Water Baptism

The Bible teaches that upon conversion the new believer is to be baptized in water. In obedience to Christ's command, Peter told the anxious crowd on the day of Pentecost that they were to repent and be baptized. Throughout the book of Acts, this commandment was carefully followed by the early church.

The significance of water baptism cannot be overemphasized. This baptism is a burial of the old self with its slavery to sin, and a resurrection into newness of life in Christ. It is an outward sign of an inward change of motivation, loyalties and affections. It is also a visible and public declaration that the newborn Christian will no longer follow the world's ways, his or her old life of sin, nor the temptations of the devil.

Mark 16:16
   Who does Christ say will be saved?

___

___

Acts 2:38
   What instructions for salvation did Peter give to the convicted crowd in Jerusalem?

___

___

Read Romans 6:3-7
   a) Verse 3. What happens when you are baptized into Christ Jesus?

___

   b) Verse 4. What is baptism associated with?

___

___

   c) Verse 5. Identifying with Christ's death means we will also be identified with what?

___

   d) Verses 6,7. What should be the result of baptism according to these verses?

___

___

___

1 Corinthians 12:13
   What are you baptized into?

___

*If you have not been baptized already, you should make arrangements as soon as possible in full obedience to Christ's command.*

*You will want to fill out the Certificate of Baptism. See* **REGISTRY**

31

## Memorize

1 John 1:8-9

## Recommended Reading

1. Alleine, Joseph. *An Alarm to Unconverted Sinners.* Grand Rapids: Baker Book House, 1979.

2. Finney, Charles G. *Instructions to Young Converts.* Belfast: Revival Movement Association.

# Memoranda

Date this chapter was completed: _____

Signature: _____

Date this chapter was reviewed with helper: _____

Helper's Signature: _____

## Chapter Two
# Community of Believers

"God never intended His church to be a refrigerator in which to preserve perishable piety. He intended it to be an incubator in which to hatch out converts."

—F. Lincicome

"So we, being many, are one body in Christ,
and every one members one of another."
(Romans 12:5)

"The church is the select company of the redeemed."
—Odin K. Stenberg

"I can more easily see our Lord sweeping the streets of London than issuing edicts from its cathedral."
—Dick Sheppard

# The Church Is the Body of Christ

Upon conversion every true follower of Jesus becomes a member of the universal and eternal body of Christ. This body or church is not a building, denomination or institution. It is a living and active organism made up of different members, fully dependent on the "head," which is the Lord Jesus Christ. Because Christ is no longer on the earth in a visible way, the church is to represent Him so the world will know and understand what He is like.

Each part or member of the body has a specific ability, purpose and calling. Every member is important, no matter how seemingly insignificant. Now that you have become a Christian, you are a vital part of this body, and your role is essential. God purposely designed the church in this manner.

Though there are many parts that make up the body of Christ, nevertheless it is one body. Christ and the early disciples prayed for and taught that there was to be a unity of all believers. Just as the eye cannot work properly apart from the hand or the rest of the physical body, no one member can operate independently of another. Together we all complement each other so the body will function properly and effectively.

Ephesians 1:20-23
   What is the church called?

_____

Ephesians 4:15
   Who is the head of the church?

_____

Romans 8:15-16
   How do you know you are part of God's family?

_____

_____

Romans 12:5
   According to this verse we are members of what?

_____

Matthew 18:20
What does God promise when we meet together?
_____
_____

1 Corinthians 12:27
What are Christians called in this verse?
_____

What are some other terms used to describe the church?

1 Timothy 3:15 _____

Ephesians 2:22 _____

Ephesians 2:20-21 _____

1 Peter 2:5 _____

1 Peter 5:2 _____

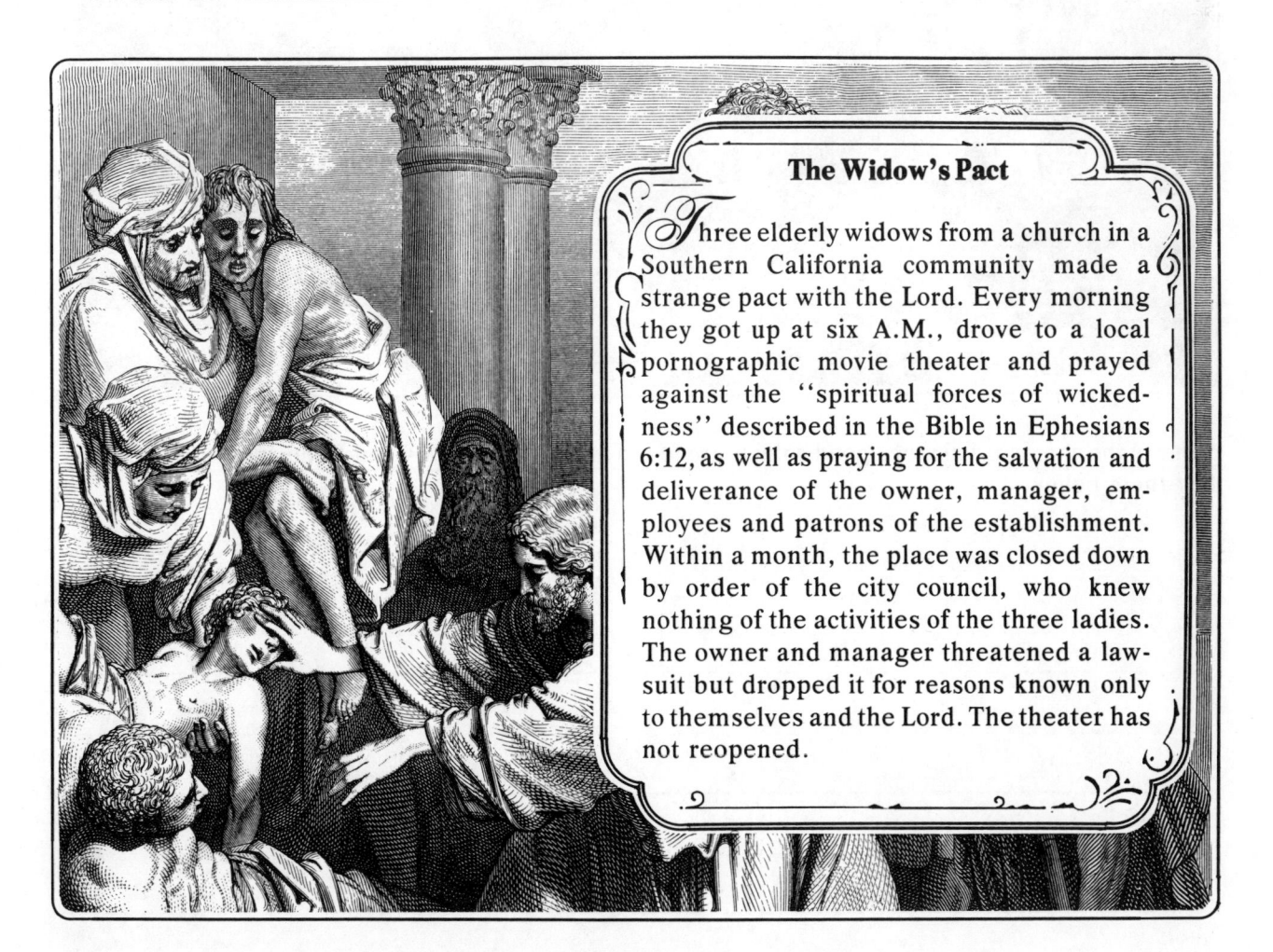

### The Widow's Pact

Three elderly widows from a church in a Southern California community made a strange pact with the Lord. Every morning they got up at six A.M., drove to a local pornographic movie theater and prayed against the "spiritual forces of wickedness" described in the Bible in Ephesians 6:12, as well as praying for the salvation and deliverance of the owner, manager, employees and patrons of the establishment. Within a month, the place was closed down by order of the city council, who knew nothing of the activities of the three ladies. The owner and manager threatened a lawsuit but dropped it for reasons known only to themselves and the Lord. The theater has not reopened.

# The Church Is the Army Triumphant

We must all remember that a spiritual war exists. It is a violent conflict between the forces of darkness and the forces of light. Every Christian, as a member of the church, is called to active full-time service as a soldier in this war.

In the Bible, God has revealed wonderful truths regarding the church's ultimate victory in this battle. Jesus said, "The gates of hell shall not prevail against it" (the church). The kingdom of darkness will not be able to stand against the might and power of the triumphant church.

We, as soldiers of the church, must direct our attack against the enemy by evangelizing the world and discipling converts of Christ. We must rescue the lost from the bondage of sin and Satan, and then train these new disciples to do the same. This should be one of the primary objectives of the church today. Every activity or program that is initiated should have this important commission in mind.

Some of the characteristics of a good soldier are found in 2 Timothy 2:3-4 and Ephesians 6:13-18. List them below.

_____    _____
_____    _____
_____    _____
_____    _____
_____    _____
_____    _____

Whom is the battle directed toward according to Ephesians 6:11-12?

_____

_____

_____

What kind of authority did Jesus give His church according to Luke 10:19?

_____

_____

### Something to Abolish

A healthy church kills error and tears evil in pieces. Not so very long ago our nation tolerated slavery. Philanthropists endeavored to destroy slavery, but when was it utterly abolished? It was when Wilberforce roused the church of God, and when the church of God addressed herself to the conflict.

I have been amused with what Wilberforce said the day after they passed the Act of Emancipation. He merrily said to a friend when it was all done: "Is there not something else we can abolish?" That was said playfully, but it shows the spirit of the church of God. She lives in conflict and victory; her mission is to destroy everything that is bad in the land.—Moody

# The Church Is Community

Jesus Christ not only desires that we be committed to Him as the "head" of the body, but also to one another as individual members of that body. To do this, we must join with other Christians who are committed to glorifying Christ through doing His will. This commitment must be evidenced by a genuine lifestyle that is visible to all, and not merely by a show of religious catchwords spoken to outwardly impress.

Christ said that the world would believe the gospel only if His followers loved one another. We must no longer think in terms of "me" but of "we." The Bible says, "A threefold cord is not quickly broken." As a community, the church must provide for the needs of others, reaching out to the poor and fatherless as well as the widowed and elderly. Jesus taught the importance of clothing the naked and feeding the hungry, visiting the sick and those in prison. By this practical display of love, a caring, dedicated and self-sacrificing community of believers can show the world what the kingdom of God is really like.

Philippians 2:3-4
  As members of the body, how should we treat each other?

Romans 12:10
  How can you personally apply this Scripture with other members of the church?

Galatians 6:2
  What does this passage mean to you?

James 1:27
   How does the Bible define true religion?
   _____
   _____

Matthew 25:34-40
   In what practical ways can we display our love for Christ?
   _____
   _____
   _____
   _____
   _____
   _____

Acts 4:32, 34, 35
   What is the great blessing of the church being a community?
   _____
   _____
   _____

Hebrews 6:10
   What is the blessing of ministering to the saints?
   _____
   _____

### The Power of Unity

Fire will not last long in a single coal, but if many coals are joined together, it will be a long time before that fire dies out. Although a traveller may not find much shelter from a single tree, he will rest comfortably beneath the thick branches of a grove. So will Jesus often sit longer where many of "the trees of the Lord" are planted.

Go to the assemblies of the saints if you would keep the arm of the King of saints. Those who dwell most with the daughters of Jerusalem are most likely to have a goodly share of Emmanuel's company. —Famous Old Preacher

# The Church Is Orderly

For the church to effectively accomplish its purpose on the earth, God has appointed specific offices that are filled according to His calling. Through apostles, prophets, evangelists, pastors and teachers, the members of the body will be equipped for the work of service and built up in the faith. In the local church there are also elders who have the responsibility of overseeing the continued growth and progress of each member. These spiritual leaders are not to be new babes in Christ, but mature and stable Christians with practical experience in ministry. It is of vital importance that they also maintain a high standard of godliness in their own homes as an example to the believers and the world.

Members of the church must lovingly and willingly submit themselves to the leaders God has placed over them. Not only does the Bible speak of members receiving instruction and encouragement, but also correction as necessary. In matters of discipline the church is to take extreme caution and care when dealing with members who have fallen into sin. If not, the church will lose its purity and power. The Bible gives specific instructions on how to take care of such cases. The execution of discipline is to be done with great love and concern, always with the intention of restoring the fallen member to right standing with God and others. Such correction will act as a strong deterrent to future sin and will show everyone the seriousness of allowing it to continue.

God has given much freedom in deciding the methods used in coordinating the daily functions of the local church. He does, though, command that it be done in such a way that it will be effective in its efforts and an example in its labors.

Read Ephesians 4:11-13.

a) What types of ministries did Christ appoint over His church?

b) What are these ministries to do?

    c) What will be the results and benefits if these ministries function properly?

What other type of leadership did Christ set up in His church according to Acts 14:23?

What are the responsibilities of the elders (Acts 20:28; Hebrews 13:17)?

What are the proper steps to take when dealing with a brother or sister who has sinned? Read Matthew 18:15-17 and write out the instructions as you understand them in your own words.

1 Corinthians 5:9-13
    How should we deal with a "so-called" brother who persists in living in sin?

James 5:19-20
    What are some of the benefits of watching out for one another?

# The Church Is Local

Though the body of Christ is universal, it is visible mainly at the local level. Paul wrote to churches throughout Asia, and Christ gave specific instructions to local churches in the book of Revelation. It is also understood in the Scriptures that upon becoming a Christian, every believer should become part of a local body. Now that you have become a Christian, it is important for you to quickly find and commit yourself to a local church that teaches and acts according to Biblical principles.

The church will function effectively only to the degree that its members are dedicated to Christ and to one another. William Carey, a shoemaker, understood what it was to be a true part of the body of Christ. When told by another to stick to his business rather than be so concerned for lost souls he replied, "My business is to work for God. I only make and mend shoes to pay my expenses." Our commitment must be one of wholeheartedness and loyalty to actively help in every way possible to see the vision, goals and strategies of the church thoroughly accomplished. Beware that our personal involvement is never halfhearted, occasional and carried out only when convenient. Indifference, negligence and selfishness will greatly hinder the work, and will put a stranglehold on every activity directed toward reaching the world for Christ. Faithful members should be able to identify with Christ's statement, "Greater love hath no man than this, that a man lay down his life for his friends" (John 15:13). Jesus was speaking in this passage to His disciples—the early church.

The importance of investing our time, talents and possessions for the work of the church can never be overemphasized. Contrary to popular belief that a tenth of all we have belongs to God, Jesus stated that a person was to give up all and follow Him. Everything we have and are comes from God and belongs to Him. This simply means that in heart attitude and action we are always ready to give anything that is needed for the advancement of the kingdom of God on earth and in heaven. Keep in mind that in the early church most gave sacrificially and not just out of their abundance.

The Bible says that God loves a cheerful giver. All that we have should be given faithfully, joyfully and sacrificially. Considering all things in light of eternity, every member counts this as a great honor and privilege for the cause of Christ.

Hebrews 10:24-25
   How do we know that Christians should meet together?

   _____
   _____

Read 1 Corinthians 12:14-21 and carefully answer the following questions.

   a) What makes up the body?

   _____
   _____

   b) Give some reasons why you are needed in the body.

   _____
   _____
   _____

   c) Can different members function on their own?

   _____ Why? _____
   _____

---

### Fire Makes the Difference

There was a blacksmith once who had two pieces of iron which he wished to weld into one. He took them just as they were, all cold and hard, and putting them on the anvil, began to hammer with all his might. But they were two pieces still and would not unite. At last he remembered what he should have never forgotten; he thrust both of them into the fire, took them out red-hot, laid the one upon the other, and by one or two blows of the hammer they very soon became one.

I remember as a child, whenever the fire truck went by, everyone would follow it to the site of the fire. But I also remember that whenever the ice-truck went by no one would follow it. It's just a simple fact that people go where there is a fire. Shouldn't our churches be filled with the fire of the Holy Spirit?—Selected.

---

1 Corinthians 4:15-16
   a) What did Paul mean by this verse?

   _____
   _____

   b) Who is your spiritual "father" (the person who led you to Christ)?

Name _____

Address _____

Phone Number _____

---

*Now fill out the Biographical Sketch of the person who led you to Christ. See* REGISTRY

*Also fill out the Biographical Sketch of the person helping you through this text. See* REGISTRY
*If your helper is your spiritual "father" it is not necessary to fill out this second sheet.*

Ephesians 5:27
   What kind of church is Christ coming back for? Write it in your own words.

_____

_____

_____


Acts 20:35
   What is Jesus saying here about giving?

_____

_____


2 Corinthians 9:7; Matthew 10:8
   What should be our attitude in giving?

_____

_____

_____


Malachi 3:8-10   Read the following verses and answer the questions below.

   a) How does a person rob God?
   _____

   b) What are we commanded to do?
   _____

   c) What will be the result of obeying God?
   _____

d) What will happen if we disobey?

_____

e) Besides tithes, what else should we give?

_____

Luke 6:38
What happens when we give to God?

_____

Deuteronomy 16:17
How much should we give?

_____

To whom should we give? Match the following Scriptures with the correct individual(s).
Matthew 5:42; Romans 12:20; Matthew 19:21; Malachi 3:8-10; Romans 12:13; Numbers 18:21,24

a) God _____   d) the person who asks _____

b) the poor _____   e) other Christians _____

c) ministers _____   f) your enemies _____

*Now turn and fill out the Certificate on "My Home Church."*  See REGISTRY

## Memorize

Romans 12:5

## Review From Memory

1 John 1:8-9

# Personal Prayer

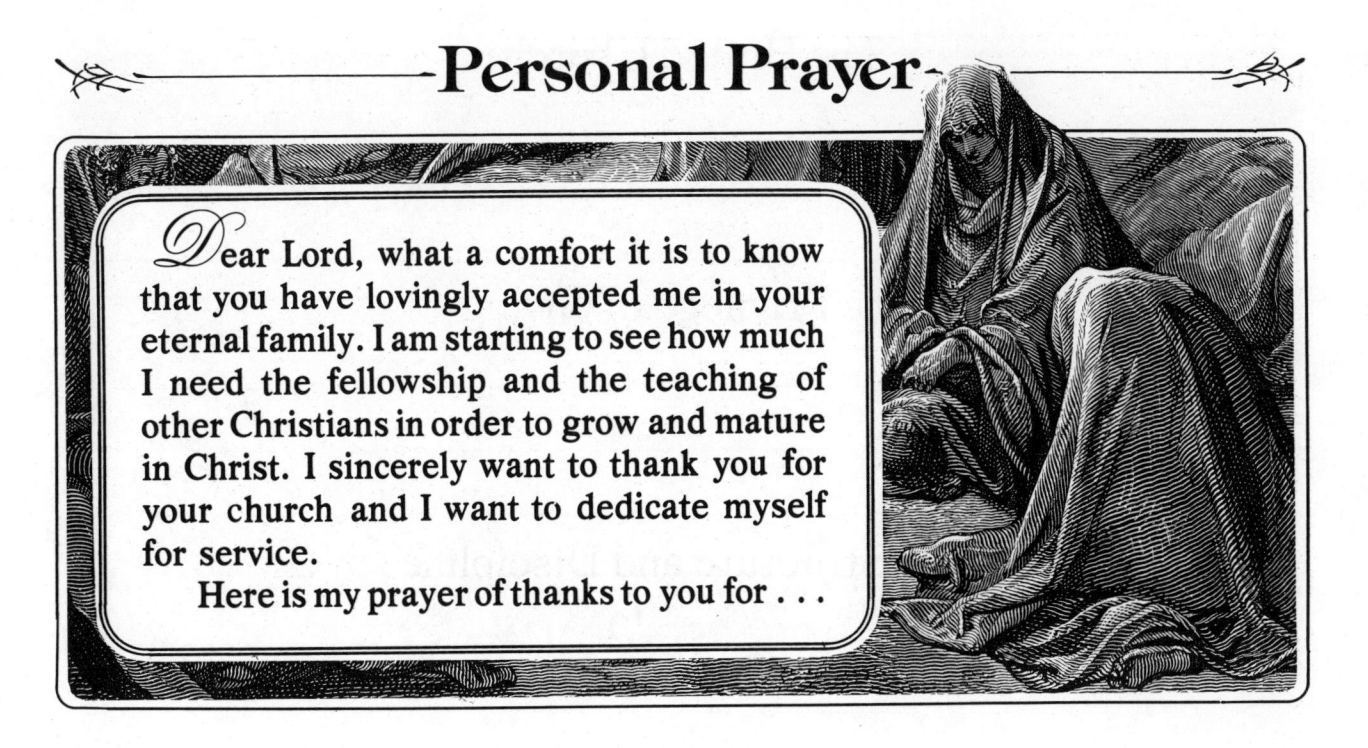

*Dear* Lord, what a comfort it is to know that you have lovingly accepted me in your eternal family. I am starting to see how much I need the fellowship and the teaching of other Christians in order to grow and mature in Christ. I sincerely want to thank you for your church and I want to dedicate myself for service.

Here is my prayer of thanks to you for . . .

### The Body of Christ

_____
_____

### The Purpose of the Church

_____
_____

### The Triumphant Army

_____
_____

### The Head of the Church

_____
_____

## The United Church

## The Privilege of Giving

## The Structure and Discipline

# Recommended Reading

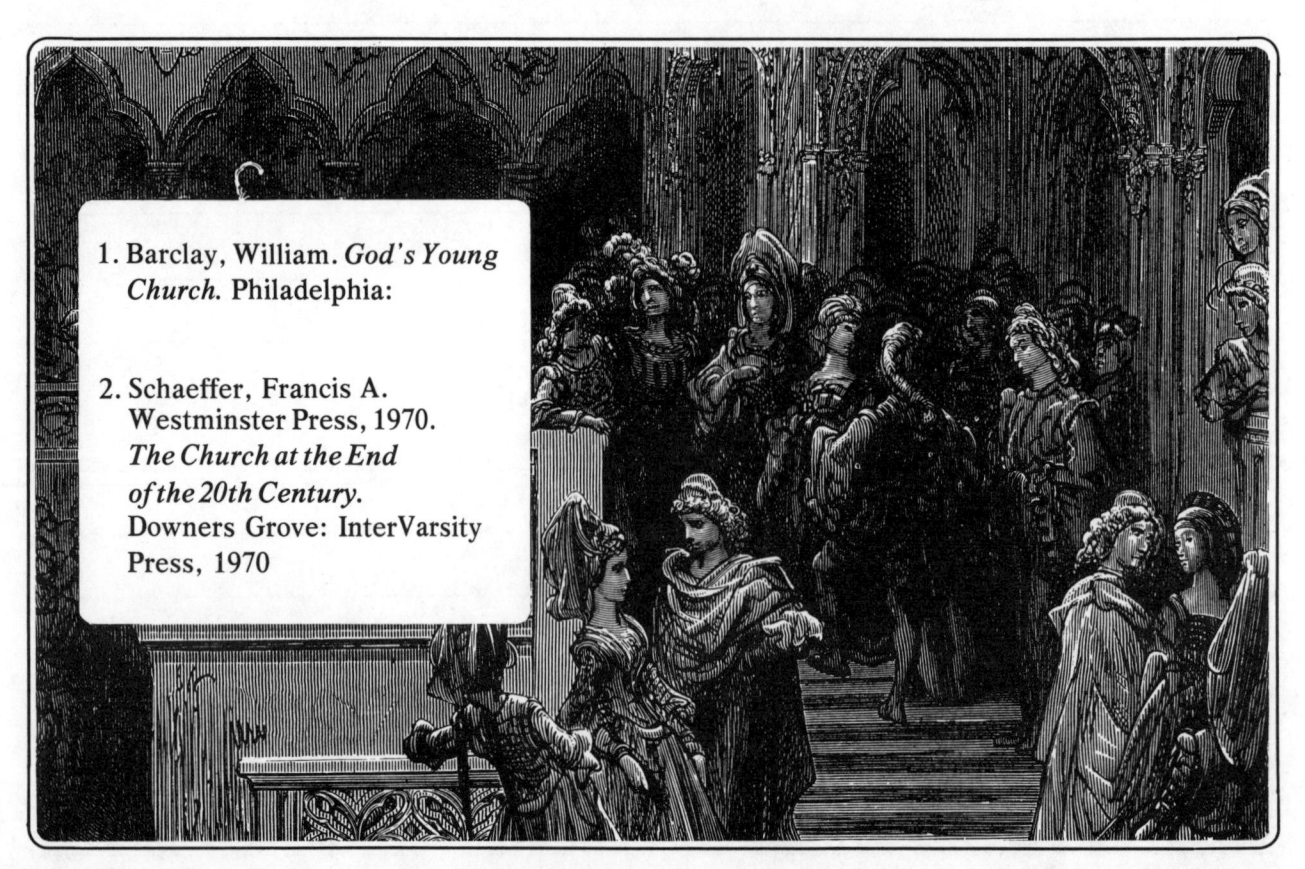

1. Barclay, William. *God's Young Church.* Philadelphia:

2. Schaeffer, Francis A. Westminster Press, 1970. *The Church at the End of the 20th Century.* Downers Grove: InterVarsity Press, 1970

# Memoranda

Date this chapter was completed: _____

Signature: _____

Date this chapter was reviewed with helper: _____

Helper's Signature: _____

# Chapter Three
# SWORD of the SPIRIT

"Reading without reflecting is like eating without digesting."
—Edmund Burke

The apostle Paul compared new believers to "babes in Christ" in need of milk to drink before they could take solid food. He considered the Corinthians as spiritually immature when he found jealousy and strife among them—signs they were still in need of instruction in the basics of the faith.

We all need to learn the basics of the Word of God, the "milk" of the Word.

We can take increasing delight in it as we find one part of Scripture connecting, strengthening, giving added meaning or clarification to another.

"I felt constrained to take the Word of God alone as my guide. Night and day for a considerable time I did little else than search the Scriptures until finally, I was so solidly grounded I have no shadow of doubt since." —Jonathan Goforth

### Baby's Feeding Himself

You know it is always regarded a great event in the family when children learn to feed themselves. They are propped up at the table, and maybe at first they use the spoon upside down, but eventually it is used correctly, and mother or sister claps her hands and says:

"Look, baby's feeding himself!"

Well, what we need as Christians is to be able to feed ourselves. There are many who sit helpless and indifferent with open mouths, hungry for spiritual things, and the minister has to try to feed them, while the Bible is a feast prepared into which they never venture.—Moody

"For the word of God is quick, and powerful, and sharper than any two edged sword, piercing even to the dividing asunder of soul and spirit, and of the joints and marrow, and is a discerner of the thoughts and intents of the heart."
(Hebrews 4:12)

# Read God's Word

*B*efore coming to Christ, the reading of the Bible is usually found uninteresting or neglected altogether. But upon conversion, it is treasured. To grow as a new believer and mature as His follower, you will want to discipline yourself to read it daily. It is not a hard book to understand and learn from if the Holy Spirit is invited to be your guide and teacher. As you read and practice principles of meditation in God's Word, you will see your life transformed by Jesus Christ, the author and perfector of your faith.

Proverbs 1:23
   What is God's promise to you regarding His Word?

1 Timothy 4:13
   What does this verse tell you to do?

   _____
   _____
   _____


2 Peter 1:20-21
   Why can you trust the Bible to be God's Word?

   _____
   _____
   _____


Acts 17:10-11
   What did the Bereans do with God's Word?

   _____
   _____
   _____

**Restored by God's Word**

Victor S___, a young man in his twenties, was a drug addict who had been in and out of mental institutions more times than his hazy memory could recall. "Hearing the gospel led me to salvation in Christ," he testifies, "and reading the Word of God cleared my mind of all the garbage that was in there. I was miraculously healed of all desire for drugs, with no withdrawal symptoms." God's Word has power and authority over everything we have knowingly and unknowingly allowed to come into our minds, hearts, and memories from the time we were born. We need to read God's Word every day to receive cleansing and renewal.

# Love God's Word

As a child of God, you will learn to love His Word. It is a lamp unto your feet and a light unto your path. It has been given for your benefit, and despite opposition from the devil, the world and your own flesh, you must learn to cling to it with all your heart. The amount of time you spend in the Word will be a reflection of the amount of love you have for God.

Psalm 1:1-2
In what did the Psalmist delight?

Psalm 19:10
How much did David value God's Word?

Read Psalm 119 and list different verses that display King David's affection for God's Word.

## A Walk Through God's Word

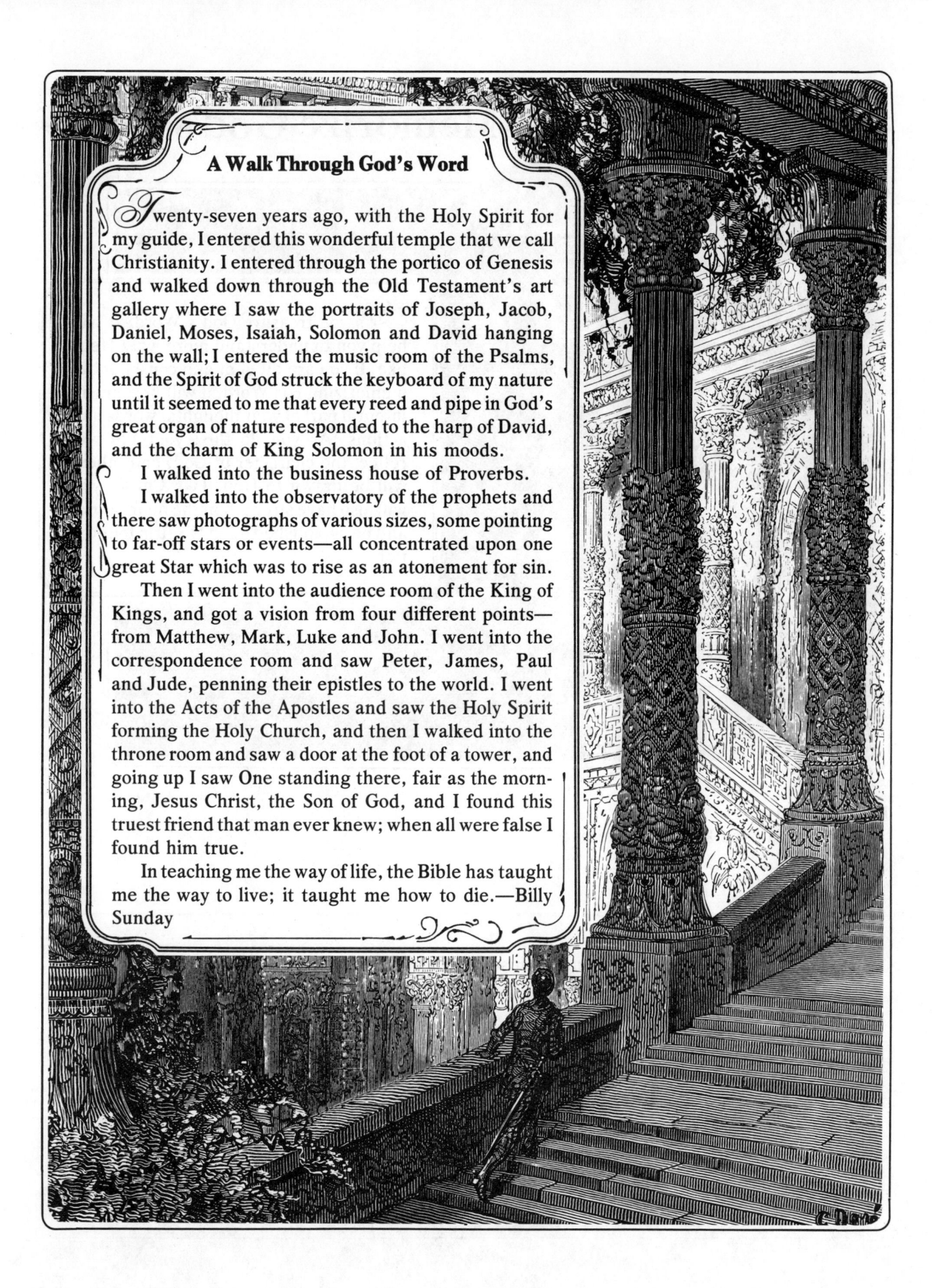

Twenty-seven years ago, with the Holy Spirit for my guide, I entered this wonderful temple that we call Christianity. I entered through the portico of Genesis and walked down through the Old Testament's art gallery where I saw the portraits of Joseph, Jacob, Daniel, Moses, Isaiah, Solomon and David hanging on the wall; I entered the music room of the Psalms, and the Spirit of God struck the keyboard of my nature until it seemed to me that every reed and pipe in God's great organ of nature responded to the harp of David, and the charm of King Solomon in his moods.

I walked into the business house of Proverbs.

I walked into the observatory of the prophets and there saw photographs of various sizes, some pointing to far-off stars or events—all concentrated upon one great Star which was to rise as an atonement for sin.

Then I went into the audience room of the King of Kings, and got a vision from four different points—from Matthew, Mark, Luke and John. I went into the correspondence room and saw Peter, James, Paul and Jude, penning their epistles to the world. I went into the Acts of the Apostles and saw the Holy Spirit forming the Holy Church, and then I walked into the throne room and saw a door at the foot of a tower, and going up I saw One standing there, fair as the morning, Jesus Christ, the Son of God, and I found this truest friend that man ever knew; when all were false I found him true.

In teaching me the way of life, the Bible has taught me the way to live; it taught me how to die.—Billy Sunday

# Memorize God's Word

As you treasure God's Word, it will help you to understand more what He is like. If you are diligent and consistent in memorizing His Word, it will become an integral part of your thoughts, words and actions. As you do this, your life will reflect the character of God, and others will be drawn to Him. Like Christ, you will also have strength in the hour of trial and be established upon His firm foundation.

Psalm 119:9,11
  a)  How can you keep your life pure?

  _____

  _____

  b)  How can you keep from sinning against God?

  _____

  _____

2 Timothy 3:14-15
What is the result of staying in God's Word?

  _____

  _____

  _____

## Wisdom Through God's Word

A young girl loved the Lord so much that she tried to get all her friends and family members to believe in Him, too. She argued with some of them for hours, without results. Discouraged, she turned to Bible study and meditation on God's Word. It wasn't long before she found herself responding to questions and comments by quoting the Bible instead of arguing in her own words. "It was different," she reported. "They wanted to know more about the Bible instead of fighting over it. My dad and mom have since given their lives to the Lord, and two of my friends are going to Bible studies. The interesting thing is that reading the Bible helps me to have a more loving attitude—and people notice it."

1 Peter 3:15
    Why should you memorize God's Word?

# Meditate on God's Word

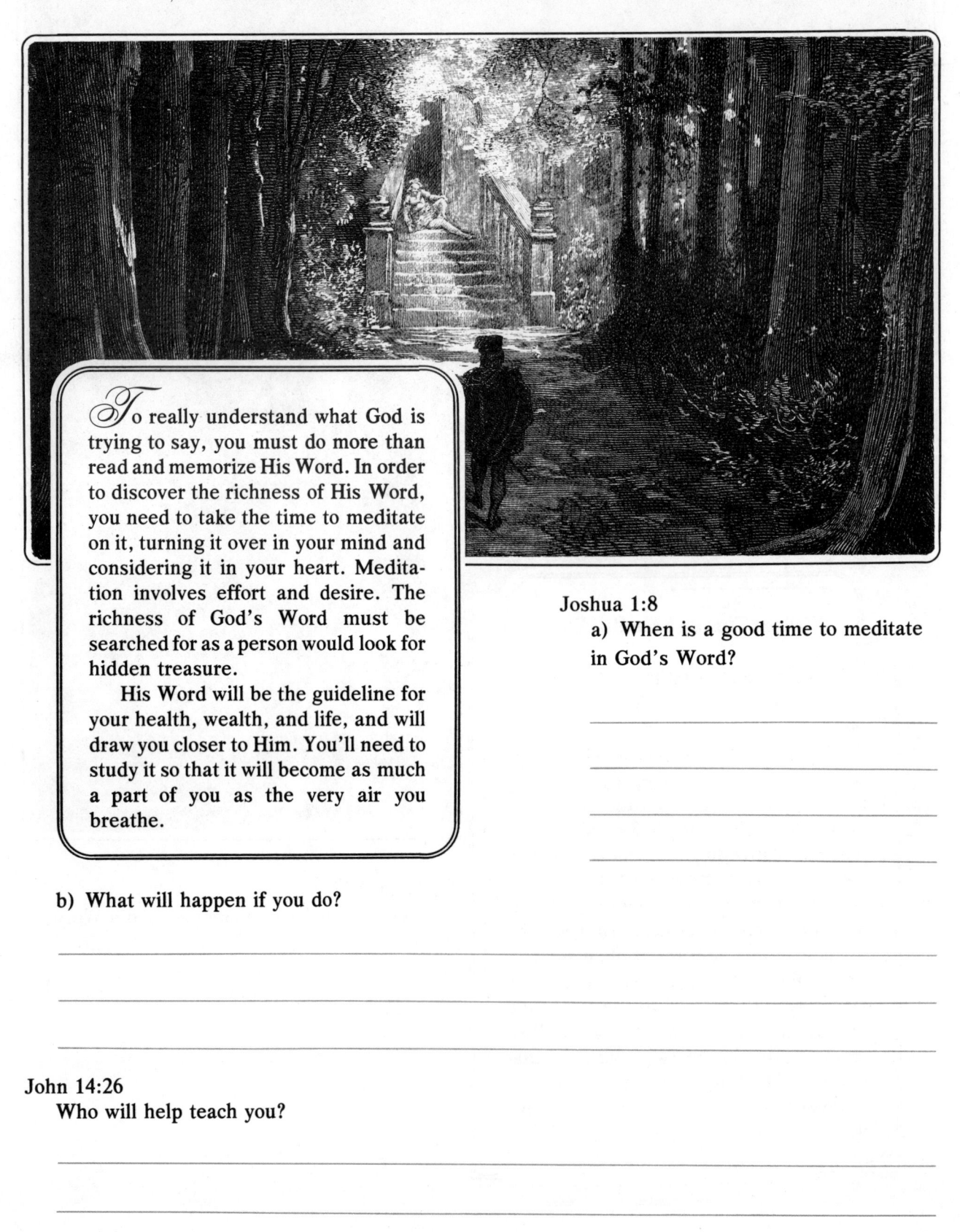

To really understand what God is trying to say, you must do more than read and memorize His Word. In order to discover the richness of His Word, you need to take the time to meditate on it, turning it over in your mind and considering it in your heart. Meditation involves effort and desire. The richness of God's Word must be searched for as a person would look for hidden treasure.

His Word will be the guideline for your health, wealth, and life, and will draw you closer to Him. You'll need to study it so that it will become as much a part of you as the very air you breathe.

Joshua 1:8
a) When is a good time to meditate in God's Word?

_____
_____
_____
_____
_____

b) What will happen if you do?

_____
_____
_____

John 14:26
Who will help teach you?

_____
_____

2 Timothy 3:16-17
   Why is it important to meditate in God's Word?

_____

_____

_____

List some things that come as a result of meditation:

Joshua 1:8 _____

Psalm 1:2-3 _____

Psalm 63:5-6 _____

Psalm 119:9,11 _____

Psalm 119:98 _____

Psalm 119:99 _____

Psalm 119:165 _____

Proverbs 16:22 _____

Romans 10:17 _____

1 Timothy 4:15 _____

> *Few books can stand three readings. But the Word of God is solid, it will stand a thousand readings, and the person who has gone over it the most frequently and the most carefully is the surest of finding new wonders there.*
> —Hamilton

# Obey God's Word

As you read the Bible and listen to God speaking through it, you'll recognize that He desires His Word to be kept. He is asking you to obey His commands because He loves you. And if you love Him, you'll keep His commands because that is what He wants. He knows they are always best for you; if you keep them, you will be happy, and He will be pleased.

> **Daniel Webster on the Bible**
>
> *I* have read through the entire Bible many times. I now make it a practice to go through it once a year. It is the book of all others for lawyers as well as ministers; and I pity the person that cannot find in it a rich supply of thought, and of rules for his or her conduct. It fits a person for life—it prepares them for death.

Joshua 1:7
   What is one of the results of obeying God's Word? _____

Exodus 24:7
   What should be my response to the Word of God? _____

2 Kings 23:2-3
   a) How did Josiah influence the people? _____

   b) How can you be an example? _____

Matthew 24:35
   How long will the Word of God last? _____

John 15:14
   How can you know you are a friend of Christ? _____

# Power of God's Word

In Acts 4:24-30 there is a powerful example of praying God's Word and applying it in a given situation. As mighty men and women of God have always prayed His Word, you need to do the same. There is tremendous power in God's Word. With it God spoke the universe into existence. You can receive stability because it is eternal; you can receive freedom over sin because it is truth, and you can receive strength in the face of trial because it comes from the very heart of God.

Psalm 119:49-50
   What were David's reasons for praying God's Word? _____



1 Kings 8:26
   Why did Solomon pray God's Word? _____

Acts 4:23-31
How did praying God's Word instill boldness in the persecuted church? _____
_____
_____

Isaiah 40:8
Why does the prophet Isaiah feel God's Word is important? _____
_____

Hebrews 4:12
What does this verse mean in your own words? _____
_____
_____
_____
_____
_____
_____

John 8:31,32
If you abide in God's Word, what happens?

a) _____
_____
_____

b) _____
_____
_____

c) _____
_____
_____

### The Anvil

I stood one day beside a blacksmith's door,
    And heard the anvil beat and the bellows chime;
Looking in, I saw upon the floor
    Old hammers worn out with beating years and years of time.

"How many anvils have you had?" said I,
    "To wear and batter all these hammers so?"
"Just one," said he, then said with twinkling eye,
    "The anvil wears the hammers out, you know."

So methought, the anvils of God's word—
    Of Jesus' sacrifice—have been beat upon.
The noise of falling blows was heard.
    The anvil is unharmed; the hammers are all gone.
        —Anonymous

# Teach God's Word

As you grow in your love for God's Word, you will want to share it with others. You will begin to take opportunities to live out God's Word with your family, friends and those who come into your circle of influence. If God's Word is applied in your life, and His precepts are followed, you will not only teach others what you are learning, but you will also show them what you are becoming.

**Abraham Lincoln on the Bible**

This great Book of God is the best gift which God has ever given to man, and that all things desirable for man to know are contained in.

Deuteronomy 6:6-9
   What should you do with God's Word?

   _____
   _____
   _____
   _____
   _____
   _____

2 Timothy 3:16,17
   God's Word is useful for so many things. List some found in these Scriptures.

   a) _____

   b) _____

   c) _____

   d) _____

   e) _____

   f) _____

Ezra 7:10
   Why should I be like Ezra?

   _____
   _____
   _____

71

# Further Insights on How to Meditate

*Learning* from God's Word is not hard because the Holy Spirit helps you. A few basic principles must be learned and the Bible will become a gold mine from which you will continually receive treasure.

## I. Learn to Read the Bible in a Variety of Ways.

A. Read the Bible in the context of the surrounding verses and then in the greater circle of the surrounding chapters, books, and the Bible as a whole.

B. Read with the literal meaning in mind unless the context indicates the words are symbolic or are a word picture.

C. Usually when the Bible repeats something, it emphasizes its importance.

D. The Bible never contradicts itself. If something seems contradictory, read the verse in light of all other verses on the same subject.

## II. Learn to Study the Bible.

    A. This will require more discipline and time than reading. The Holy Spirit will help and teach you if you ask Him.

    B. Gather the basic materials for a study: a concordance, a Bible, a notebook and a pen or pencil. (Always record your studies in a notebook to help remember them and to refer to them in the future.)

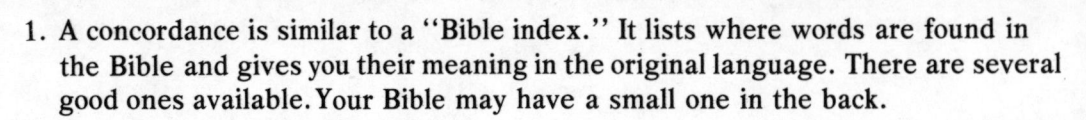

1. A concordance is similar to a "Bible index." It lists where words are found in the Bible and gives you their meaning in the original language. There are several good ones available. Your Bible may have a small one in the back.

2. Use a good translation of the Bible, such as the *King James Version* or the *New American Standard*.

C. Here is a sample of one kind of simple basic study using the verse Joshua 1:8, the *Strong's Exhaustive Concordance* and the *King James Version*.

1. Read the first chapter of Joshua to begin to understand the context of who is speaking and what the topic is. (Make a mental note to be sure to read the entire book!)

2. Head the page of your notebook, possibly titling it "Study on Joshua 1:8", and write out verse 8.

## Study on Joshua 1:8

Joshua 1:8 "This book of the law shall not depart out of thy mouth; but thou shalt meditate therein day and night, that thou mayest observe to do according to all that is written therein: for then thou shalt make thy way prosperous, and then thou shalt have good success."

3. You may want to look up the word "meditate" in the *Strong's Concordance*. You will find it listed alphabetically.

   a) All the verses where the word "meditate" is used in the Bible will be listed.

   b) The reference numbers in the right hand column, (i.e., 1897, 7878, 3191, 4304) indicate where the original Hebrew and Greek words are listed in their respective dictionaries in the back of the *Strong's Concordance*.

   c) **Make a note of the reference number for Joshua 1:8, "1897." This reference number will identify the original Hebrew** word and its definition which has been translated "meditate."

   d) Look up number 1897. It is found in the "Hebrew and Chaldee Dictionary" in the back of the *Strong's Concordance* on page 32.

   e) You will find the original word means "to *murmur* (in pleasure or anger); by implication to *ponder.*" Any other words listed are the various ways this word is translated and appears in other verses in the *King James Version*.

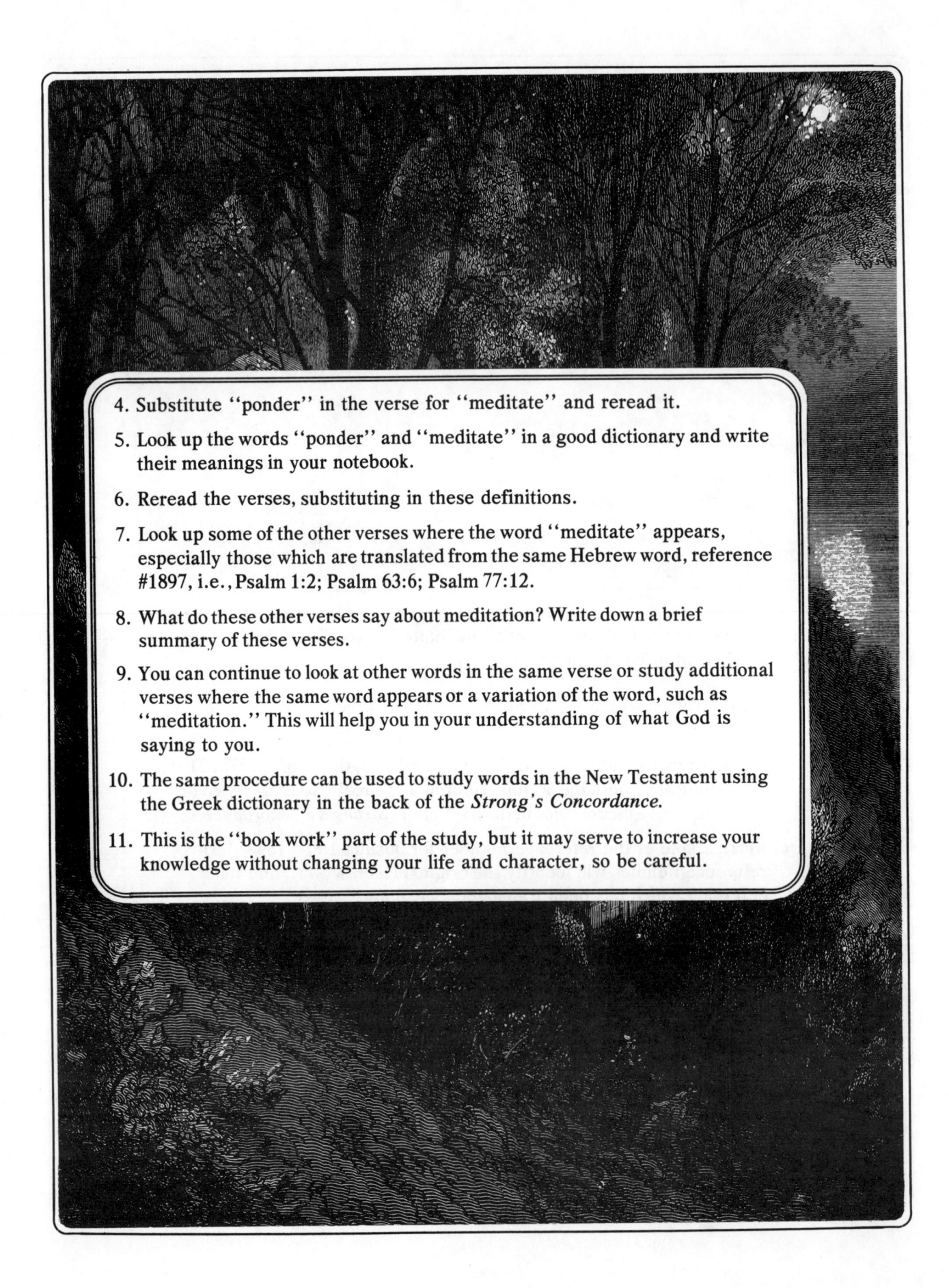

4. Substitute "ponder" in the verse for "meditate" and reread it.

5. Look up the words "ponder" and "meditate" in a good dictionary and write their meanings in your notebook.

6. Reread the verses, substituting in these definitions.

7. Look up some of the other verses where the word "meditate" appears, especially those which are translated from the same Hebrew word, reference #1897, i.e., Psalm 1:2; Psalm 63:6; Psalm 77:12.

8. What do these other verses say about meditation? Write down a brief summary of these verses.

9. You can continue to look at other words in the same verse or study additional verses where the same word appears or a variation of the word, such as "meditation." This will help you in your understanding of what God is saying to you.

10. The same procedure can be used to study words in the New Testament using the Greek dictionary in the back of the *Strong's Concordance*.

11. This is the "book work" part of the study, but it may serve to increase your knowledge without changing your life and character, so be careful.

# III. Learn to Live God's Word.

A. If you are a true follower of Christ, you will want God's Word to live in your heart. So remember what the Hebrew word for meditate means. You will need to ponder God's Word and act on the principles learned.

B. Read the verse aloud and to yourself several times. This repetition will help you to remember the verse through habit just like dialing a telephone number until it becomes familiar!

C. Think about what God is instructing you to do. Ask yourself questions: "What am I supposed to do? What is the resulting promise for me? How will this verse affect my daily life? How will it make me love God more?"

D. God's Spirit may speak and ask you to do something. You need to act on whatever He shows you to do.

# IV. Learn to Pray God's Word.

It is most important when meditating upon a verse or a passage of Scripture to personalize it and make it a prayer to God.

A. Proverbs 28:5 "Evil men understand not judgment: but they that that seek the LORD understand all things."

B. Personalize it:
   If I am evil I will not know how to make wise decisions, but if I will seek the Lord I will understand all things.

C. Pray it:

Dear Heavenly Father, I am beginning to understand the difference between an evil person and a wise person. If I am wicked I will not know how to make good and fair decisions. But as I seek you and meditate in your Word I will learn all things. I have made many foolish mistakes, and now I understand why— because I have not sought you. I want to learn to follow you and learn from you so that my life will please you and bring great glory to your name.

# Memorize

Proverbs 30:5

## Review From Memory

1 John 1:8-9

Romans 12:5

# Personal Prayer

*Realizing* the importance of daily reading and meditating in the Bible, write out a prayer to God involving your personal commitment and loyalty to His Word.

# Recommended Reading

1. McAlpine, Campbell. *Alone With God.* Minneapolis: Bethany Fellowship, 1981.

2. Baxter, J. Sidlow. *Explore the Book.* Grand Rapids: Zondervan Publishing House, 1979.

# Memoranda

Date this chapter was completed: _____

Signature: _____

Date this chapter was reviewed with helper: _____

Helper's Signature: _____

Chapter Four

# Life-Breath of the Soul

"Reading one hundred expositions about prayer will never equal one vital experience of prayer."
—L. Ravenhill

When you give your life to the Lord you are a "new creature" in Christ. As a newborn Christian and a member of His body, it is important to eat and drink of God's Word for daily growth. To meditate in the Holy Scriptures gives wisdom and strength and brings great joy, but there is more . . .

"The prayers of God's saints are the capital stock in heaven by which Christ carries on His great work upon earth."
—E.M. Bounds

"I sought to hear the voice of God and climbed the topmost steeple; But God declared: Go down again—I dwell among the people." —John Henry Newman

### Divine Prayer

God respecteth not the arithmetic of our prayers—how many they are; nor the rhetoric of our prayers—how neat they are; nor the geometry of our prayers—how long they are; but the divinity of our prayers—how heart-sprung they are.—Haines

"The effectual fervent prayer of a righteous man availeth much." (James 5:16)

# The Life-Breath of the Soul Is Prayer

> There is something else that must be done to maintain a healthy, happy and growing relationship in our new lives. It's the secret of power; it's the most intimate approach to God; it's the channel by which all spiritual blessings are received. Of course, you know what it is—prayer.

Read Daniel 6
   a) How important was prayer to Daniel?

   b) What happened because He prayed?

   c) How can I apply this to my life?

### Save the Students!

When a professor of Hamilton College lay on his death bed, his doctor whispered to the professor's wife, "Your husband is dying." The old man heard and looked up with a smile on his face and asked, "Did I understand you to say that I am dying?"

Sadly the doctor said, "Yes, I'm sorry, you have no more than half an hour to live."

The old professor smiled again. "Then it will soon be over," he said. "Take me out of bed and put me on my knees. I want to die praying for the students of Hamilton College." They lifted him out and he knelt down and covered his face with his transparent hands and prayed, "Oh, God, save the students of Hamilton College."

For a time he continued to pray, then the doctor said, "He is getting weaker." They lifted him back on the bed, and his face was whiter than the pillows. Still his lips moved. "Oh God, save—" Then the light of life went out, and he finished the prayer in the presence of Jesus. What did his dying prayer do? Why, almost the entire student body of Hamilton College accepted Jesus Christ.

1 Thessalonians 5:17
How important should prayer be in my life?

# The Battle Is Won in Prayer

While prayer should be easy to do, it isn't always. There is nothing the enemy of the soul will try to stop more than prayer. He knows well that this is the vital link to heaven. It is the lifeline to the Almighty God. All great men and women of God have always regarded prayer as the most important business of their lives, and it is necessary for all of us to do the same. Even though the devil doesn't want us to pray, our Heavenly Father greatly desires it and will help us overcome all obstacles.

Genesis 32:24-30

   a) Why did Jacob wrestle with the angel? _____

   b) What principle of prayer is shown in this passage? _____

List seven individuals in the Bible who prayed. Also list specific things that were accomplished through their prayers.

| | Individual | Specific things that were accomplished through prayer. |
|---|---|---|
| 1) | _____ | _____ |
| 2) | _____ | _____ |
| 3) | _____ | _____ |
| 4) | _____ | _____ |
| 5) | _____ | _____ |
| 6) | _____ | _____ |
| 7) | _____ | _____ |

## Men of Prayer

Every man and every woman that God has used to halt this sin-cursed world and set it going Godward has been a Christian of prayer. Martin Luther arose from his bed and prayed all night, and when the break of day came he called his wife and said to her, "It has come." History records that on that very day King Charles granted religious toleration, a thing for which Luther had prayed.

John Knox, whom his queen feared more than any other man, was in such agony of prayer that he ran out into the street and fell on his face and cried, "Oh, God, give me Scotland or I'll die!" And God gave him Scotland, and not only that, he threw England in for good measure.

When Jonathan Edwards was about to preach his greatest sermon on "Sinners in the Hands of an Angry God," he prayed for days; and when he stood before the congregation and preached it, men caught at the seats in their terror. Some fell to the floor. The people cried out in their fear, "Mr. Edwards, tell us how we can be saved!"

The critical period of American history was between 1784 and 1789. There was no common coinage, no common defense. When the colonies sent men to a constitutional convention, Benjamin Franklin, rising with the weight of his four score years, asked that the convention open with prayer, and George Washington there sealed the bargain with God. In that winter in Valley Forge, Washington led his men in prayer and he got down on his knees to do it.

When the Battle of Gettysburg was on, Lincoln, old Abe Lincoln, was on his knees with God; yes, he was on his knees from five o'clock in the afternoon till four o'clock in the morning, and Bishop Simpson was with him.

Daniel 10:12-14
What was one reason why Daniel's prayer was not immediately answered?

# Jesus Sets the Example in Prayer

*Prayer* occupied a prominent place in the earthly life of our Lord. By spending time with His Father, we find that His strength was renewed and His wisdom increased. Frequently He would slip away to find a quiet place alone in the wilderness to pray and return with greater power and burning compassion for all humanity.

It is not, therefore, unusual that we should find that this is still an important part of His present ministry.

Luke 11:1
What did the disciples ask Jesus to do and why is this important for you to know?

_____
_____
_____

What different things do these Scriptures show us about Jesus' prayer life?

    Matthew 14:23 _____

    Mark 1:35 _____

    Mark 6:46 _____

    Luke 6:12 _____

What is Jesus doing for us now?

    Romans 8:34 _____

    Hebrews 7:25 _____

## Praying Parents

*I* went to lunch with John G. Paton, a missionary to the New Hebrides. One day he said to me, "All that I am I owe to my Christian father and mother. My father was one of the most prayerful men I ever knew. Often in the daytime he would slip into his closet, and he would drop a handkerchief outside the door, and when we children saw the white sentinel we knew that father was talking with his God and would go quietly away. It is largely because of the life and influence of that same saintly father that I am preaching to the cannibals in the South Seas."

It is an insult to God and a disgrace to allow children to grow up without throwing Christian influences around them. Seven-tenths of professing Christians have no family prayers and do not read the Bible. It is no wonder boys and girls are going to hell.—Billy Sunday

# We Must Learn the Importance of Prayer

*It* is God's desire that we should spend the rest of our lives learning to make prayer an active and practical part of our daily walk with Him. With His help there is nothing that can or will stop us from this important task. We must devote our hearts to prayer as well as our time and energy. Without it, our relationship with God will be severely hindered and our effectiveness as Christians will be diminished. We must be confident that God will teach us secrets to prayer that will help us to be fervent and productive, resulting in much accomplished for His glory. This is His will for all of us and we need to be diligent in pursuing it.

Write out some Scriptures that describe the following kinds of prayer.

**Thankfulness:** Scripture Reference _____

Write out verse _____

### Just Like Him

$\mathcal{R}$esemblance to God results from our intimacy with Him. We soon assume the manners of those with whom we are familiar, especially if we love and revere them. Upon this principle, the more we have to do with God, the more we shall grow into His likeness and "be followers of Him as dear children."—Jay

**Praise:** Scripture Reference _____

Write out verse _____

_____

_____

_____

_____

_____

**Petition:** Scripture Reference _____

Write out verse _____

_____

_____

_____

_____

_____

**Intercession:** Scripture Reference _____

Write out verse _____

_____

_____

_____

_____

_____

**Adoration:** Scripture Reference _____

Write out verse _____

_____

**Travailing:** Scripture Reference _____

Write out verse _____

_____

_____

**In the Spirit:** Scripture Reference _____

Write out verse _____

_____

## These Are Some Things for Which I Can Pray:

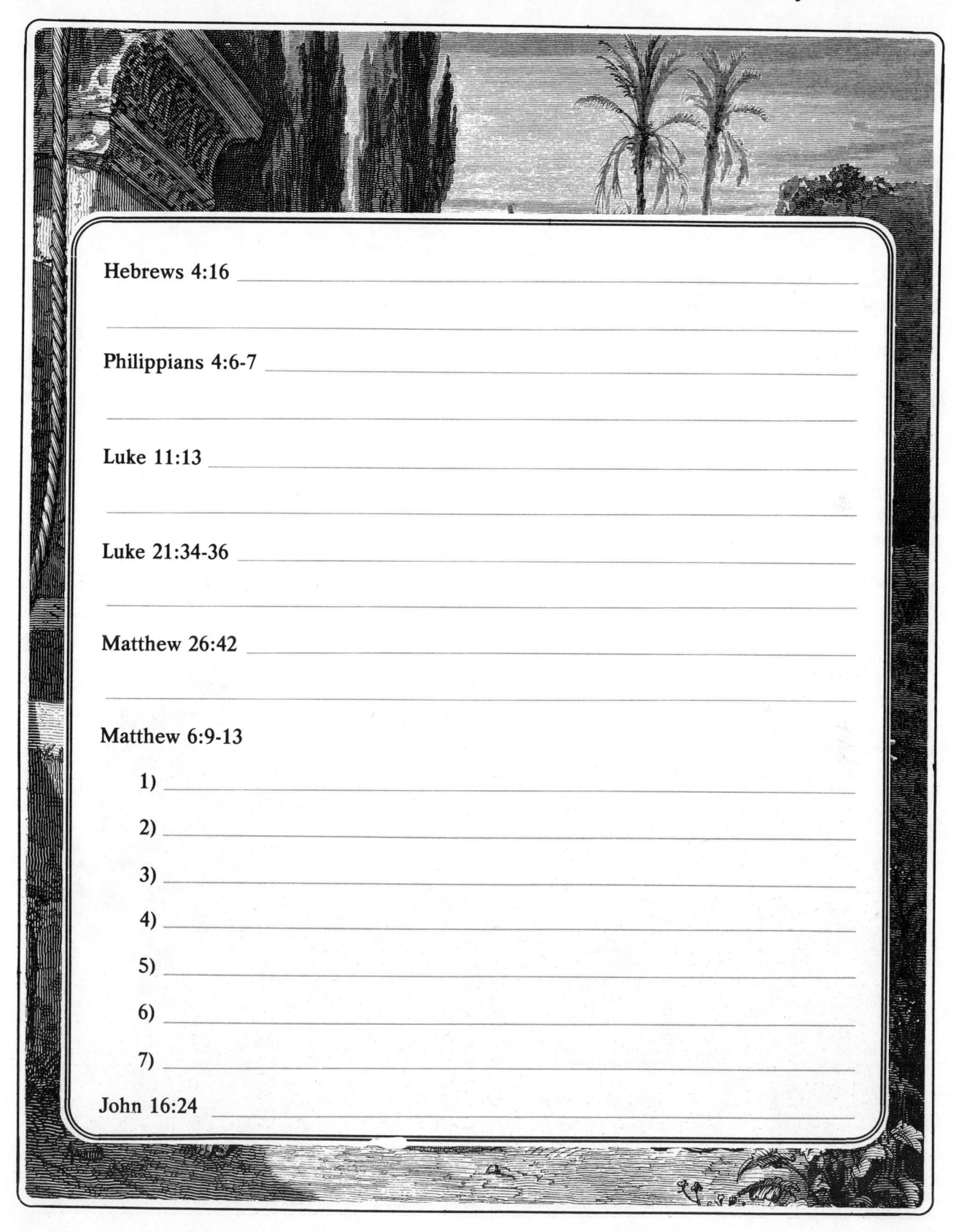

Hebrews 4:16 _____

Philippians 4:6-7 _____

Luke 11:13 _____

Luke 21:34-36 _____

Matthew 26:42 _____

Matthew 6:9-13

    1) _____

    2) _____

    3) _____

    4) _____

    5) _____

    6) _____

    7) _____

John 16:24 _____

# Other Things for Which I Can Pray:

**Write where each verse is found in the Bible. Also write how each of these verses can personally relate to you.**

"... pray for them which despitefully use you"     Scripture Reference _____

I can pray for ... _____

_____

"Pray ... the Lord of the harvest, that
he will send forth laborers into his harvest."     Scripture Reference _____

I can pray for ... _____

_____

"... pray always, that ye may be accounted
worthy to escape all these things that shall come
to pass, and to stand before the Son of Man."     Scripture Reference _____

I can pray for ... _____

_____

"... pray one for another,
that ye may be healed ..."     Scripture Reference _____

I can pray for ... _____

_____

*You may now want to review or start your "Journal of Prayer."* See **REGISTRY**

**Can You Find Other Things for Which the Bible Tells Us to Pray?**

Scripture Reference I can pray for . . .

# Some Ways the Scripture Shows Me to Pray

## 1. Pray in secret:

"But thou, when thou prayest, enter into thy closet, and when thou hast shut thy door, pray to thy Father which is in secret; and thy Father which seeth in secret shall reward thee openly." (Matthew 6:6)

What does this mean to you? _____

_____

_____

## 2. Pray specifically:

"And when he heard that it was Jesus of Nazareth, he began to cry out, and say, Jesus, thou son of David, have mercy on me. And Jesus answered and said unto him, What wilt thou that I should do unto thee? The blind man said unto him, Lord, that I might receive my sight. And Jesus said unto him, Go thy way; thy faith hath made thee whole. And immediately he received his sight, and followed Jesus in the way." (Mark 10:47,51,52)

Give examples of praying specifically: _____

_____

_____

_____

## 3. Pray boldly:

"Let us therefore come boldly unto the throne of grace, that we may obtain mercy, and find grace to help in time of need." (Hebrews 4:16)

What does it mean to me to pray boldly? _____

_____

_____

_____

## 4. Pray persistently:

"And he said unto them, Which of you shall have a friend, and shall go unto him at midnight, and say unto him, Friend, lend me three loaves; For a friend of mine in his journey is come to me, and I have nothing to set before him? And he from within shall answer and say, Trouble me not: the door is now shut, and my children are with me in bed; I cannot rise and give thee. I say unto you, Though he will not rise and give him, because he is his friend, yet because of his importunity he will rise and give him as many as he needeth. And I say unto you, Ask, and it shall be given you; seek, and ye shall find; knock, and it shall be opened unto you. For every one that asketh receiveth; and he that seeketh findeth; and to him that knocketh it shall be opened." (Luke 11:5-10)

What is the lesson I can learn here? _____

_____

## 5. Pray according to the will of God:

"Ye ask, and receive not, because ye ask amiss, that ye may consume it upon your lusts" (James 4:3). "And this is the confidence that we have in him, that, if we ask anything according to his will, he heareth us: And if we know that he hear us, whatsoever we ask, we know that we have the petitions that we desired of him." (1 John 5:14,15)

How do I apply this to my life? _____

_____

## 6. Pray in faith:

"But let him ask in faith, nothing wavering. For he that wavereth is like a wave of the sea driven with the wind and tossed. For let not that man think that he shall receive anything of the Lord." (James 1:6,7)

From now on when I pray... _____

_____

## 7. Pray in the name of Jesus:

"And whatsoever ye shall ask in my name, that will I do, that the Father may be glorified in the Son." (John 14:13)

How should I pray? _____

_____

## 8. Pray with a pure heart:

"Behold, the Lord's hand is not shortened, that it cannot save; neither his ear heavy, that it cannot hear: But your iniquities have separated between you and your God, and your sins have hid his face from you, that he will not hear." (Isaiah 59:1,2)

What will keep the Lord from hearing me? _____
_____
_____
_____

## 9. Pray fervently:

"Confess your faults one to another, and pray one for another, that ye may be healed. The effectual fervent prayer of a righteous man availeth much." (James 5:16)

What kind of prayer will be effective? _____
_____
_____

## Memorize

1 Thessalonians 5:16-18

## Review From Memory

1 John 1:8-9

Romans 12:5

Proverbs 30:5

# Personal Prayer

> Write out below your own personal prayer to the Lord specifically using any of the principles you have just learned. An example is given below.

**Principle:** Pray Specifically

Dear Lord, I thank you for your Holy Spirit that brings conviction to a person's heart. You know that I have been witnessing to the young man that lives next door to me and he is really starting to listen. Give me wisdom to say the things that will lead to his conversion. Continue to work in his life and bring about situations that will show him that you are real and love him very much.

Principle: _____

Principle: _____

Principle: _____

Principle: _____

# Recommended Reading

1. M'Intyre, D.M. *The Hidden Life of Prayer.* Grand Rapids: Baker Book House, 1979.

2. Morgan, G. Campbell. *The Practice of Prayer.* Grand Rapids: Baker Book House, 1971.

# Memoranda

Date this chapter was completed: _____

Signature: _____

Date this chapter was reviewed with helper: _____

Helper's Signature: _____

## Chapter Five
# Knowledge of the Holy One

"I know nothing which can so comfort the soul; so calm the swelling billows of sorrow and grief; so speak peace to the winds of trial, as a devout musing upon the subject of the Godhead."
—C.H. Spurgeon

"Those who know God have great energy for God." —J.I. Packer

"As God is the only perfect being in the universe, His character consisting of all that is good and great, must be the model of all human excellence..."
—Noah Webster

As Christians, we will spend all eternity with God. It is important to understand that He is the most valuable and loving Being in the entire universe. Because of this, we will want to dedicate the rest of our lives to this all important objective: to know and love Him. The following are some fundamental truths about God we all need to learn.

**"That the God of our Lord Jesus Christ, the Father of glory, may give unto you the spirit of wisdom and revelation in the knowledge of him." (Ephesians 1:17)**

# God Is the Triune, Eternal Creator

The Bible teaches that there is only one God and no other. He is the great Creator of the earth and universe, uncreated Himself, having always existed throughout eternity. He is wonderfully revealed in the Bible as a Supreme Being consisting of three awesomely great persons unified in one. Though distinct from each other, these divine persons (the Father, the Son and the Holy Spirit) nevertheless share an absolute oneness in substance, essence and nature that is emphasized through the Bible.

The Bible also speaks of God's ability to think and reason, to feel and experience deep emotions and to make choices from His creative powers. As God created us in a limited likeness of His own great Being, when we think, feel or choose, we are given a glimpse of what God Himself must be like.

What important facts do we learn about God from the following verses?

a) Psalm 90:2     Psalm 102:27     Isaiah 57:15

_____

b) Deuteronomy 4:35     Isaiah 43:10     Ephesians 4:6

_____

c) Genesis 1:26     Genesis 3:22     John 17:22

_____

Who is called God in the Scriptures?

a) 2 Peter 1:17 _____

b) Titus 2:13 _____

c) Acts 5:3-4 _____

What are some of the results of knowing God?

a) Proverbs 9:10 _____

b) John 17:3 _____

c) Daniel 11:32 _____

## Playing Hooky

I want to tell you a little story. Many years ago my two boys, then small, were going to school. Both of them are now preachers. One is in this country, an American citizen, doing evangelistic work, the other son is in England, a minister.

Well—my two boys, when they were young, were sent to school. They had what I didn't. I gave them the opportunity to get what I missed in my childhood. One day they came home unusually early for lunch. They came at 11:30, when they should not have been at home until 12:30. They had not been to school, I knew. They had played, as you say in America, hooky. In England, we call it playing truant. I was a very young father. My first boy was born before I was twenty-one. I felt it my duty to do something about the matter. I took my watch out and said, "Boys, why are you home so soon? Where have you been?"

"We have been playing," they said.

"Yes, playing truant."

They admitted it.

"I have never played truant in my life," I said.

"You never went to school," the elder boy said.

"No," I said, "I did not. I did not have your chance. My not having attended school was a misfortune; your not having attended is a sin."

I knew they must be punished, but I didn't know how to go about it. I was a very young and inexperienced father. I was up against it, to use one of your American "classic" phrases. I had to do something. I shrank from the idea of punishing them. It was harder for me in truth than for them.

"You will have to be punished," I said. I sent the elder boy upstairs to the back room and told him to stay there all day. Then I sent the other boy to another room, and bade him do likewise.

"You will have bread and water for dinner and for supper and nothing else," I told them.

When dinner-time came, I took them up their bread and water. I couldn't trust anyone else. Albany, the elder, ate his and asked for more. Hanley did not touch his, and I need not tell you who are parents that I did not eat that day. No food would have tempted me. And I cannot tell you how often I climbed those stairs to see what the boys were doing. I could not read, or write, or see people. It was the first time in my life that anything had come between my boys and myself. And my young father-heart suffered far more than the boys. I was punished most, because love suffers.

At night-fall I was listening on the landing, and found Albany had entered into rest and was snoring. Hanley could not sleep. He was already penitent. Hearing my footsteps, he called me: "Daddy! Will you forgive me just this once and I will never play truant any more!" I grabbed him, bedclothes and all, and hugged him to my heart. I tried to kiss back his tears, and mine got mingled with his. I told him it was all forgiven and passed. Then he said, "Daddy, do you love me just as much as before?" I answered, "You know I do." Then he asked, "Are you very sure?" and I answered, "Yes, Hanley dear, I am very sure." Then the child said, "Take me down to supper." In plain English the child meant, if you love me, prove it.

The Bible says, "The works of the Lord are great . . . His work is honorable and gracious: and His righteousness endureth forever. He hath made his wonderful works to be remembered: the Lord is gracious and full of compassion. He hath given meat unto them that fear him: he will ever be mindful of his covenant. He that shewed his people the power of his works . . ."

"The works of his hands are verity and judgment; all his commandments are sure. They stand fast for ever and ever, and are done in truth and uprightness. He sent redemption unto his people: he hath commanded his covenant for ever: holy and reverend is his name. The fear of the Lord is the beginning of wisdom: a good understanding have all they that do his commandments: his praise endureth for ever."

—Billy Sunday

### A Converted Woodsman

A converted woodsman gave the following reason for his belief in the Trinity: "We go down to the river in winter and we see it covered with snow; we dig through the snow, and we come to the ice; we chop through the ice, and we come to the water. Snow is water; ice is water; water is water; therefore the three are one."

# God Is an Infinite Spirit, All-Powerful, All-Knowing and Everywhere Present

God has always had unspeakably great powers. He is able to be present in all of His creation at once; the very energies of His being holding all things together. He has infinite knowledge of all things actual and possible in the past, present and future. With His limitless powers, He is capable of doing all that is pracically and morally possible.

The following scriptures teach us about God's unique attributes. Look up each verse and write what it says about Him.

a) Psalm 139:7-10 _____

b) Jeremiah 23:23-24 _____

c) Hebrews 4:13 _____

d) What does this tell us about God's presence?

_____

a) Genesis 18:14 _____

b) Job 42:2 _____

c) Matthew 19:26 _____

d) What does this tell us about God's power?

_____

a) Psalm 139:2-6 _____

b) Psalm 147:5 _____

c) 1 John 3:20 _____

d) What does this tell us about God's knowledge?

_____

### You've Got It Wrong

A Scottish woman was once introduced as "Mrs. _____, a woman of great faith."

"No," she said, "I am a woman of little faith, but with a great God."

117

# God Is Love

*Every* action that God takes and every decision that He makes is motivated by love. Throughout the Bible, the Godhead is shown to exercise great concern and care for all of humanity. He unselfishly chooses what will be best for everyone and everything. He does all things without showing favoritism to anyone. His great love is shown in His delight and desire for the welfare of all. It is often displayed in many ways, for instance the way He disciplines us and the way He suffers when we suffer.

1 John 4:16
   What fundamental truth does this verse teach you about God?

_____

Whom does God love?

a) Matthew 3:17 _____

b) John 14:21,23 _____

c) John 3:16 _____

d) Romans 5:8 _____

119

## A Mother's Love

*I* was once preaching for Dr. G. in St. Louis, and when I got through he said that he wanted to tell me a story. There was a boy who was very bad. He had a very bad father, who seemed to take delight in teaching his son everything that was bad. The father died, and the boy went on from bad to worse until he was arrested for murder.

When he was on trial, it came out that he had murdered five other people, and from one end of the city to the other there was a universal cry going up against him. During his trial they had to guard the court house, the indignation was so intense.

The white-haired mother got just as near her son as she could, and every witness that went into the court and said anything against him seemed to hurt her more than her son. When the jury brought in a verdict of guilty a great shout went up, but the old mother nearly fainted away; and when the judge pronounced the sentence of death they thought she would faint away.

After it was over she threw her arms around him and kissed him, and there in the court they had to tear him from her embrace. She then went the length and breadth of the city trying to get men to sign a petition for his pardon. And when he was hanged, she begged the governor to let her have the body of her son, that she might bury it. They say that death has torn down everything in this world, everything but a mother's love. That is stronger than death itself. The governor refused to let her have the body, but she cherished the memory of that boy as long as she lived.

A few months later she followed her boy, and when she was dying she sent word to the governor, and begged that her body might be laid close to her son. That is a mother's love. She wasn't ashamed to have her grave pointed out for all time as the grave of the mother of the most noted criminal the State of Vermont ever had.

The prophet takes hold of that very idea. He says: "Can a mother forget her child?" But a mother's love is not to be compared to the love of God.—Moody

# God Is Light

Because God is the example of perfect conduct, His own manner of living must be the standard by which we pattern our lives. To conform to what is proper in relating with others or to live up to what is right, is called "light" in the Bible. God is light because He lives in perfect accordance with what His absolute intelligence reveals as most loving. He is doing everything that is right.

The Bible teaches that we must "walk in the light, as He is in the light." This means that as God reveals to us what is right, we must accordingly act just as He does.

1 John 1:5
   What should we tell others about God?

1 John 1:7; John 8:12
   What will be the results of following God's example?

# God Is Holy

The Bible teaches us that God is absolutely pure and without moral blemish. Nothing imperfect or evil can be found in Him. The angels have always reverently declared this truth about God. The Scriptures speak of this attribute of God as holiness. One way it is revealed is by His utter hate for sin and love for righteousness. God commands us to be holy, just as He is holy.

Isaiah 6:3
   What do the angels call God in this verse?

_____

1 Peter 1:15-16
   What is God's command to us?

_____

How do these scriptures show the holiness of God?

   a) Psalm 5:4-5 _____

   _____

   b) Proverbs 15:9 _____

   _____

   c) Job 34:10 _____

   _____

   d) Isaiah 59:1-2 _____

   _____

Following God's example, what are some practical, everyday ways I can display holiness in my life?

# God Is Merciful

The Bible is full of passages that describe God as compassionate, forgiving, kind, patient, longsuffering and merciful (full of lovingkindness). These marvelous characteristics of God have been made clearly evident through His personal dealings with fallen humanity. Ever since Adam and Eve first sinned against God, He has continually extended His mercy in hopes of restoring the human race back into a right relationship with Himself. He would much rather exercise mercy than judgment.

What characteristics of God are found in Psalm 103:8?

To whom does God show mercy?

a) Romans 9:15,18 _____

b) Psalm 103:11,17 _____

c) Proverbs 28:13 _____

d) Psalm 86:5 _____

e) Isaiah 49:13 _____

Lamentations 3:22-23
How often does God exercise His mercy toward us? _____
_____

# God Is Wise

One of the greatest reasons why God can be trusted is because of His infinite wisdom. This wisdom is revealed as He uses His supreme knowledge for the purpose of bringing about the greatest good. Always knowing what the results will be of His benevolent choices, He does what is best on our behalf.

What is God called in Jude 25? _____

What was one of the accomplishments of God's wisdom found in Proverbs 3:19? _____

According to Proverbs 2:6, who gives wisdom? _____

Describe God's wisdom in Romans 11:33. _____

What is the source of true wisdom and knowledge in Colossians 2:2-3? _____

# God Is Faithful

God is totally trustworthy in all of His dealings concerning our lives. Because the Bible teaches that God is the "same yesterday, today and forever," He will always be consistent in the way He loves and cares for everyone. Even though we may not have been completely faithful to Him in the past, God's Word assures us that He has never changed in His absolute faithfulness toward us. Therefore, there is no reason to ever doubt or mistrust Him.

How does Deuteronomy 7:9 describe God?

_____

_____

Of what does 2 Timothy 2:13 assure us regarding God's faithfulness?

_____

How does God display His faithfulness in the following verses?

    a) Psalm 89:20-26 _____

    b) Psalm 89:33-34 _____

    c) Psalm 119:75 _____

    d) Psalm 143:1 _____

    e) 1 Corinthians 10:13 _____

    f) 2 Thessalonians 3:3 _____

    g) 1 John 1:9 _____

List some specific ways God has been faithful to you:

1. _____

2. _____

3. _____

4. _____

5. _____

6. _____

7. _____

130

## Full Nets

Not long after Peter, the fisherman, met Jesus, he took Him out on his boat a little off shore on Lake Gennesaret to preach to a crowd that had gathered. Afterward, Jesus said to him, "Go out to the deep water and let down your nets." Peter, no doubt, was irritated. He knew Jesus was an authority on spiritual matters, but now the Lord was treading on his specialty—fishing. "Master, we worked all night and caught nothing," he said, "but at your word I'll let down the net." When he did, the nets were immediately so full of fish that another boat had to come help. Both boats were filled, almost to the point of sinking. Stunned, Peter fell at Jesus' feet, saying, "Depart from me—I am a sinful man, Lord!"

God is faithful to meet all our needs as we put Him first in our lives. If you have failed in some area of your life, put Jesus first and give it another try. See what Jesus puts in your net.

8. _____

# God Is Righteous

The righteousness of God is shown in the Bible by His acts of love, guided by truth, in relationship to all people. This can also be termed justice. The two words "righteousness" and "justice," are often paralleled in the Scriptures. This characteristic of God always leads Him to do what is lawful and right.

God's righteousness can be closely linked to His holiness, but they are not exactly the same. Holiness refers to God's character, while righteousness is evidenced by His dealings with others. Since God always does what is lawful and right, He hates all evil.

2 Chronicles 12:6
   What did the people of Israel say about the Lord?

Psalm 11:4-7
   How does God display His righteousness?

1 John 3:7
   What does God command us to do?

# Memorize

John 17:3

# Review From Memory

1 John 1:8-9

Romans 12:5

Proverbs 30:5

1 Thessalonians 5:16-18

# Personal Prayer

*What a marvelous God we serve! Knowledge of Him is too wonderful to comprehend. Write out a prayer of thankfulness for the many awesome and wonderful attributes of God. After you have finished writing this out, humbly and sincerely pray it to Him.*

God Is Love:

_____
_____
_____

God Is Light:

_____
_____
_____

God Is Holy:

_____
_____
_____

God Is Merciful:

God Is Wise:

God Is Faithful:

God Is Righteous:

## Recommended Reading

1. Jones, E. Stanley. *The Unshakable Kingdom and the Unchanging Person.* Nashville: Abingdon Press, 1972.

2. Otis, George Jr. *The God They Never Knew.* Milford: Mott Media, 1982.

3. Packer, J.J. *Knowing God.* Downers Grove: InterVarsity Press, 1973.

# Memoranda

Date this chapter was completed: _____

Signature: _____

Date this chapter was reviewed with helper: _____

Helper's Signature: _____

## Chapter Six
# HEART of GOD

"We are not made for law, but for love."  —George Macdonald

Since God has restored you to a right relationship with Him, you should be learning the value of His Word and the power of prayer. One of the things you will begin to notice more and more about God as you grow in the knowledge and understanding of His character is His tremendous love. The following are some principles you need to learn about His love so that you will become more like Him.

"Love multiplies rapidly. It is a divine and delightful contagion, a heavenly leaven."  —K. Neill Foster

"The primary qualification for a missionary is not love for souls, as we so often hear, but love for Christ." —Vance Havner

"Beloved, let us love one another: for love is of God; and every one that loveth is born of God, and knoweth God." (1 John 4:7)

# Love Is From God

God's love is immeasurable. All of us have, at some time or another, taken this love for granted, bringing Him much grief and sorrow. It is humbling to realize that, even while we rejected God, He never changed in His love toward us. He has shown His love to us in various ways, although many times we have not been aware of it. His care and protection have been unceasing; His blessings have been numerous; His forgiveness has been final and His remembrance has been constant.

When Jesus came to the earth He demonstrated God's love by suffering and dying in our place. He told His disciples, "Greater love hath no man than this, that a man lay down his life for his friends." This act of love is the basis for our salvation. Without it, we would have no hope.

Read the following Scriptures and list some ways in which God displays His love toward you:

| Reference | Ways God Displays His Love |
| --- | --- |
| Deuteronomy 32:9-14 | |
| Hebrews 12:5-11 | |
| Isaiah 63:9 | |
| 1 John 4:9-10 | |
| Isaiah 49:15-16 | |
| Isaiah 55:7; 38:17 | |
| Ephesians 2:4-7 | |
| Zephaniah 3:17 | |
| 1 John 3:1 | |
| Deuteronomy 7:6-13 | |
| Jeremiah 31:3 | |

## A True Test

A little boy came to his father and laid his hand upon his knee, looking up attentively. "Do you want a penny, son?" the father asked. The sweet face glowed, and the answer came: "No, Daddy, only you."

So it is with the child of God. He does not want the good things of the world nor even a small portion of it so much as he wants to know his Father's love. This is a true test for each of us, and by it we may know whether we are really in the faith.—Frances E. Willard

# Love Is the Greatest Commandment

People have often been interested in what God considers the most important command. One day a religious leader asked Jesus a question regarding this. Instead of naming one of the Ten Great Commandments which the leader might have supposed, Jesus referred to the greatest of all commandments. This is what He said, "You shall love the Lord your God with all your heart, and with all your soul, and with all your mind, and you shall love your neighbor as yourself." The wonderful thing is that God loves us in this same way, so we are simply imitating His love in obeying this command.

We cannot allow anyone or anything to become a greater object of our love than God. To be willing to lay our lives down for our Heavenly Father should become a natural result of our love for Him.

Mark 12:28-30
Which is the first commandment of all?

_____
_____
_____

This commandment is also found in Matthew, Luke and Deuteronomy. Please find and list the scriptural references.

Matthew _____

Luke _____

Deuteronomy _____

### The Little Fellow Knows

In Chicago a few years ago, a little boy attended a Sunday School. When his parents moved to another part of the city the little fellow still attended the same Sunday School, although it meant a long, tiresome walk each way. A friend asked him why he went so far, and he told him that there were plenty of others just as good closer to his home.

"They may be as good for others, but not for me," was his reply.

"Why not?" she asked.

"Because they love a fellow over there," he replied.

If only we could make the world believe that we loved them, there would be fewer empty churches, and a smaller proportion of our population who never darken a church door. Let love replace duty in our church relations, and the world will soon be evangelized.

Matthew 22:36-40

How do we know that the Ten Commandments and all other commandments rest on the great Love Commandment?

Deuteronomy 5:7-21    List the Ten Commandments.

1. _____
2. _____
3. _____
4. _____
5. _____
6. _____
7. _____
8. _____
9. _____
10. _____

# Love Is the Base of All Commandments

1. Love to God will admit no other god.
2. Love stands against everything that debases its object by representing it with an image.
3. Love to God will never dishonor His name.
4. Love to God will reverence His day.
5. Love to parents makes one honor them.
6. Hate, not love, is a murderer.
7. Lust, not love, commits adultery.
8. Love will give, but never steal.
9. Love will not slander or lie.
10. Love's eye is not covetous.

# The Royal Law

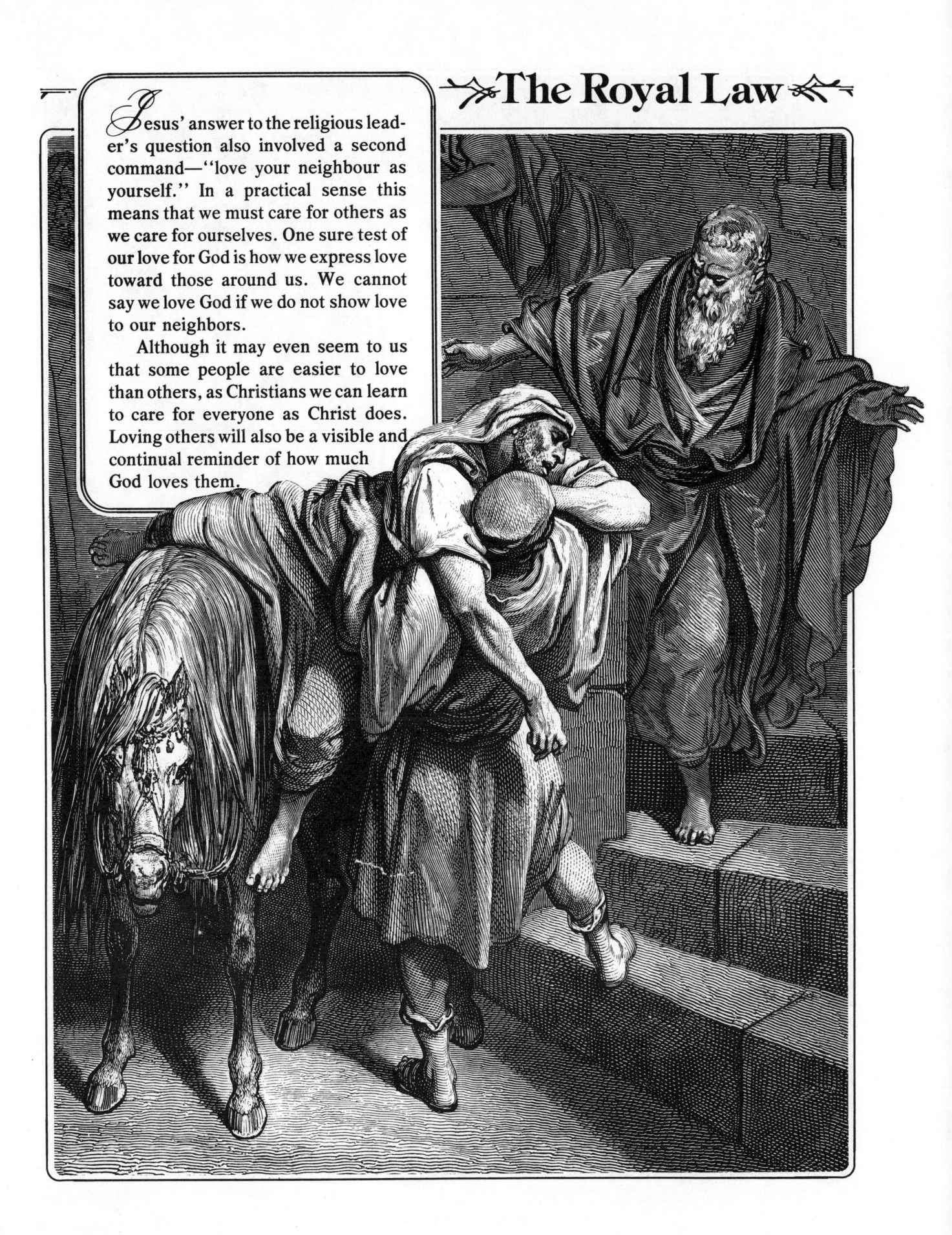

*J*esus' answer to the religious leader's question also involved a second command—"love your neighbour as yourself." In a practical sense this means that we must care for others as we care for ourselves. One sure test of our love for God is how we express love toward those around us. We cannot say we love God if we do not show love to our neighbors.

Although it may even seem to us that some people are easier to love than others, as Christians we can learn to care for everyone as Christ does. Loving others will also be a visible and continual reminder of how much God loves them.

## The Sinking Ship

Years ago there was a ship on the Atlantic when a storm arose. The ship sprung a leak. In spite of all the men did, they could not pump out the water fast enough. The captain called the men to him and told them that he had taken observations and bearings. Unless the leak was stopped, in ten hours the boat would be at the bottom of the sea. "I want a man who will volunteer his life to stay the intake. It's in the second hold. The hole is about the size of a man's arm. Someone can place his arm in the hole, and it will hold back the water until we can get it pumped out."

Not a man stirred. They said they would go back to the pumps, and they did. They worked hard. When a man dropped they would drag him away, revive him, and bring him back. The captain called them again and told them it was no use unless their strategy changed. They would be at the bottom of the sea before ten hours unless someone volunteered—in less time than that if a storm arose. Then one stepped up.

"What! My boy!"

"Yes, Father, I'll go."

He sent some endearing words to his mother and kissed his father. Then he bade the sailors goodbye, took one last look at the sky, and went below. He found the leak and placed his arm in it, packing rags around it. The men went back to the pumps. When the day broke they saw the body floating and swaying in the water, but the arm was still in the hole. And the vessel sailed into port safe. There on the coast today stands a monument to perpetuate the deed.

Nineteen hundred years ago this old world sprung a leak. God asked for volunteers to stop it. All of the angels and seraphim stood back; Noah, Abraham, Elijah, Isaiah, David, Jeremiah, Solomon, none would go, and then forth stepped His Son: "Father, I'll go," He said. And He descended and died on the cross.—Billy Sunday

1 John 4:20-21
What does the Bible say about me if I do not love my neighbor?

James 2:8
How is the Royal Law fulfilled?

This commandment to love your neighbor as yourself is found in Mark 12:31.
It is also found in

Matthew _____ Luke _____

and Leviticus _____

Luke 10:29-37
What is the Biblical definition of "my neighbor"?

Galatians 5:14
How does the Bible say we can fulfill the law?

# Love Is More Than a Feeling

The kind of love Jesus was talking about was called "agape." It is a unique kind of love: unconditional, never doing something with the hope or expectation of receiving something in return. Even though we may not feel affection toward someone, the kind of love God commands us to practice is based not primarily on feelings, but on choice. When our emotions let us down, we can still care for someone as God cares for us. Throughout the Scriptures, this pure love was visibly displayed by God, and He asks us to do the same.

Matthew 5:44
    How does this verse prove that love is more than a feeling?

1 John 3:18
   What is more important than saying that we love?
   _____
   _____

Ephesians 5:1-2
   What is God asking us to do?
   _____
   _____
   _____

John 13:34-35
   What will others know about me if I love as Christ loves?
   _____
   _____

Matthew 24:3,12
   What is a sign of the end times?
   _____
   _____
   _____

> As a fire goeth out if it be not maintained with wood, so likewise, love groweth cold which is not mixed with good works.—Cawdray

# Love Is Unselfish Benevolence

"Agape" is disinterested benevolence. The idea of disinterested or unselfish benevolence sounds complicated, but it is not. Benevolence is simply the willingness to show kindness to others.

The opposite of "agape" is selfishness—doing everything for personal gratification. God is not this way. His love knows no limits. It is always kind and is absolutely opposed to selfishness. Love is truthful, merciful, compassionate, patient and impartial. Through Christ, we must choose to do what is best for God and others even if we do not receive anything in return. This is exactly how God loves us and we must follow His example.

## Willie Lee

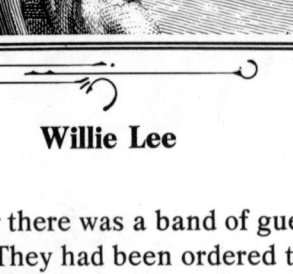

In the Civil War there was a band of guerillas called Quantrell's Band. They had been ordered to be shot on sight. They had burned a town in Iowa and they had been caught. One long ditch was dug and they were lined up in front of it, blindfolded and tied. Just as the firing squad was ready to present arms a young man dashed through the bushes and cried, "Stop!" He told the commander of the firing squad that he was as guilty as any of the others, but he had escaped and had come of his own free will. He pointed to one man in the line and asked to take his place. "I'm single," he said, "while he has a wife and babies." The commander of that firing squad, who was an usher in one of the cities in which I held meetings, told me how the young fellow was blindfolded and bound. The guns rang out and he fell dead.

Time went on. One day a man came upon another in a graveyard in Missouri. He was weeping and shaping a grave into form. The first asked who was buried there. The other said, "The best friend I ever had." Then he told how he had not gone far away, but had come back to get the body of his friend after he had been shot in order to bury it; he knew he had the right body. He had brought a withered bouquet all the way from his home to put on the grave. He was poor then, and could not afford anything costly, but he had placed a slab of wood on the pliable earth with these words on it: "He died for me."

Major Whittle stood by the grave some time later and saw the same monument. If you go there now you will see something different. The man became rich. Today there is a marble monument fifteen feet high with this inscription:

Sacred to the memory of
WILLIE LEE
He took my place in the line
He died for me

Sacred to the memory of Jesus Christ. He took our place on the cross and gave His life that we might live, and go to heaven, and reign with Him. —Selected

1 Corinthians 13 is a whole chapter on agape (charity). Go through each verse listed below and write it in your own words. Try as much as possible to personalize it. An example is given below for verse 6.

Verse 1

Verse 2

Verse 3

Verse 4

Verse 5

Verse 6 *I must never be happy over sinful actions, situations, or intentions but be very excited over truth, righteousness, and anything that pleases God.*

Verse 7

Verse 13

# Love Is Servanthood

In a day and age when being a slave was looked upon with contempt, Peter, James, Paul and other members of the early church proudly and boldly called themselves servants or slaves of God. These early disciples considered it a badge of honor and a distinguishing mark of a follower of Christ.

The term "servant" and all it implies seems harsh and offensive, but not when we realize its meaning to these faithful believers. They were love slaves! This was not forced slavery but the willing and happy slavery of love.

It is generally understood that a slave has no rights. We must recognize that upon becoming Christians those things which we consider as rights should be yielded up to Christ. In the words of Samuel Brengle:

> The love-slave is altogether at his Master's service. He is all eyes for his Master. He watches. He is all ears for his Master. He listens. His mind is willing. His hands are ready. His feet are swift. To sit at the Master's feet and look into His loved face; to listen to His voice and catch His words; to run on His errands; to do His bidding; to share His privations and sorrows; to watch at His door; to guard His honour; to praise His name; to defend His person; to seek and promote His interests, and, if needs be, to die for His dear sake, this is the joy of the slave of love, and this he counts his perfect freedom.

Mark 10:43-44
   How is greatness attained in the kingdom of God?

_____

_____


Philippians 2:5-7
   What was Jesus' attitude toward being a servant?

_____

_____

_____

1 Corinthians 9:19
   What was Paul's attitude toward being a servant?

Galatians 5:13
   What are we to do with our freedom in Christ?

Matthew 11:29
   What kind of Master do we serve?

## A Loving Spirit

In the late professor Drummond's "The Greatest Thing in the World," he tells of meeting with natives in the interior of Africa who remembered David Livingstone. They could not understand a word he uttered, but they recognized the universal language of love through which he appealed to them. It had been many years since that Christian hero passed away, but the very remembrance of his presence among them would kindle a friendly smile.

It is this very selfsame universal language of love, divine, Christ-like love, that we must have if we are going to be used of God. The world does not understand theology or dogma, but it understands love and sympathy. A loving act may be more powerful and far reaching than the most eloquent sermon.

What are some rights that can be yielded? Match the following scriptures with the corresponding right listed below.

| Right to: | Matching Scripture |
|---|---|
| 1. Home | Matthew 6:25 |
| 2. Family | 1 Thessalonians 2:4 |
| 3. Food and clothing | Matthew 19:29 |
| 4. Reputation | Proverbs 18:24 |
| 5. Life | Luke 9:57-58 |
| 6. Possessions | Mark 1:16-18 |
| 7. Friends | Matthew 6:19 |
| 8. Occupation | 1 Corinthians 6:19 |

Matthew 19:29
What are the rewards of yielding rights? _____

What rights may you possibly need to yield? _____

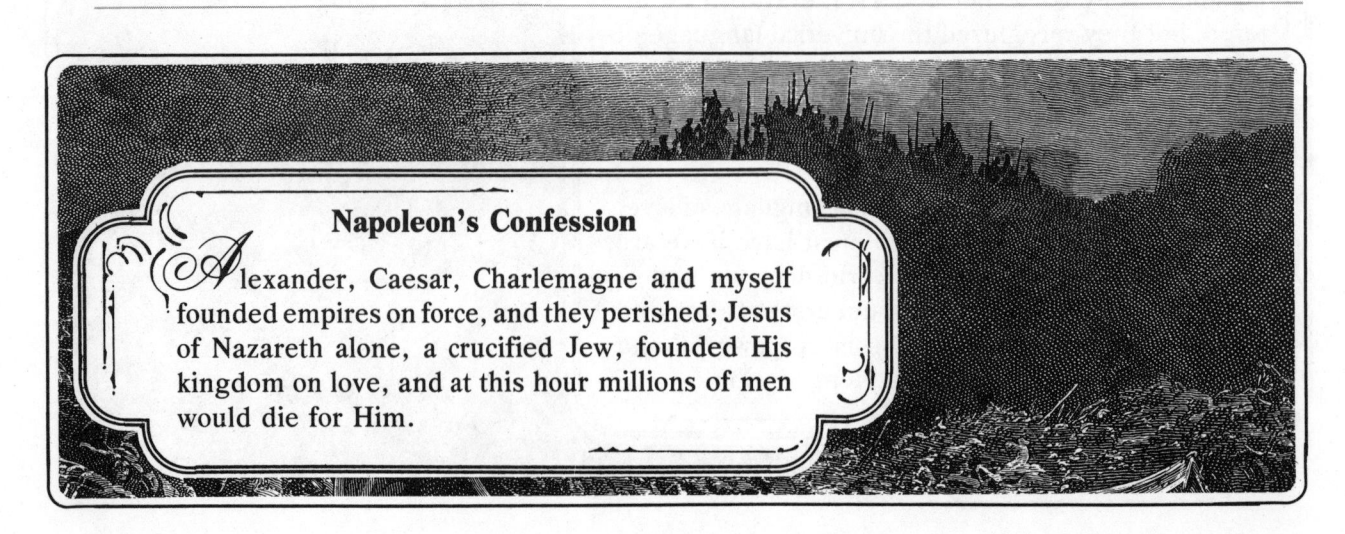

### Napoleon's Confession

Alexander, Caesar, Charlemagne and myself founded empires on force, and they perished; Jesus of Nazareth alone, a crucified Jew, founded His kingdom on love, and at this hour millions of men would die for Him.

# Exercise of Love

Here are some ways I can display true Christian love:

At home I can _____

_____

At school I can _____

_____

At work I can _____

_____

At church I can _____

_____

In my recreation I can _____

_____

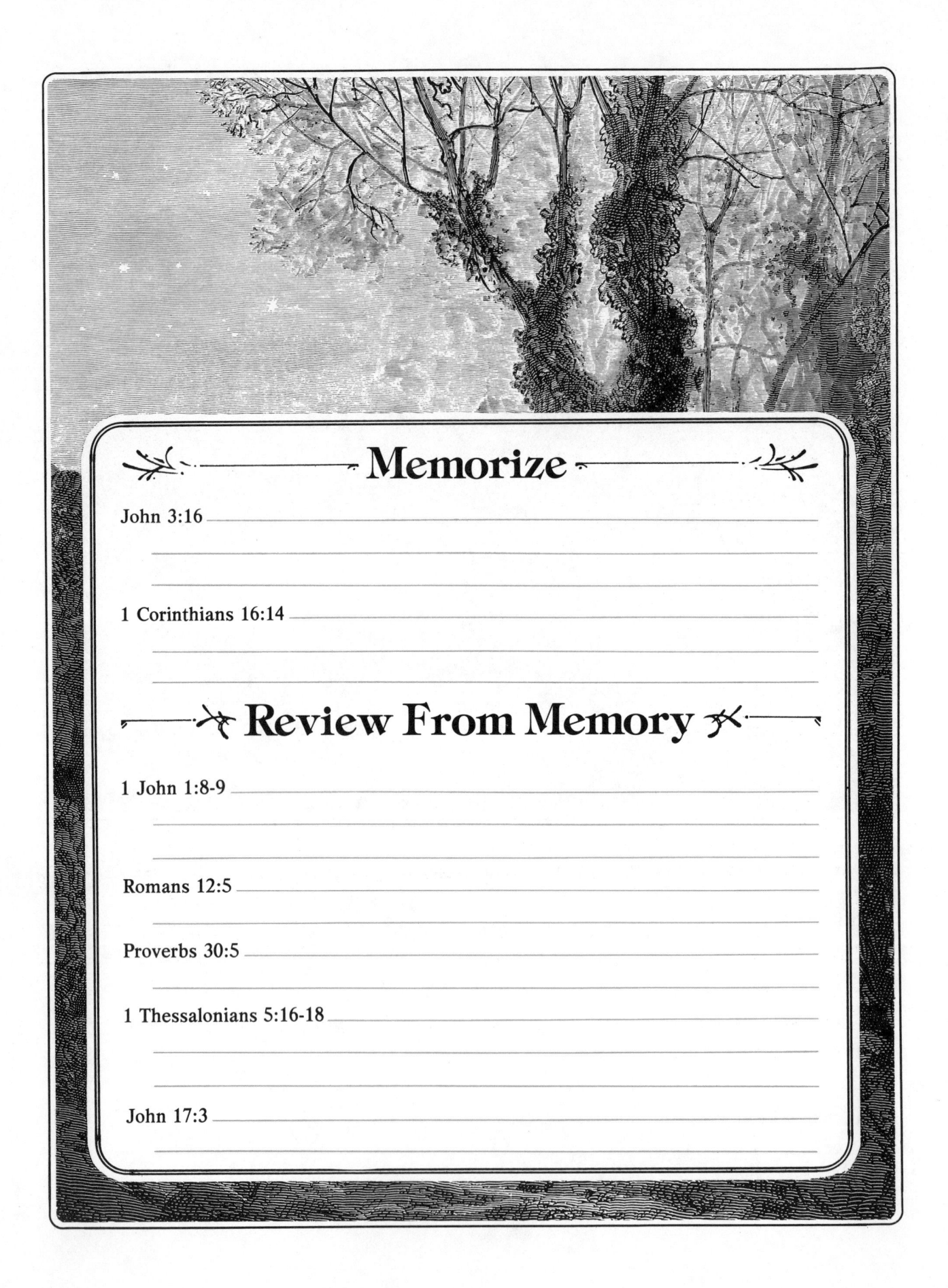

## Memorize

John 3:16

1 Corinthians 16:14

## Review From Memory

1 John 1:8-9

Romans 12:5

Proverbs 30:5

1 Thessalonians 5:16-18

John 17:3

# Personal Prayer

*Write your own personal prayer to the Lord specifically stating your intent to apply the different principles of love that you are learning about in this chapter.*

### God Loves Me

_____
_____

### Love Is the Greatest Commandment

_____
_____

### The Royal Law

_____
_____

### Love Is More Than a Feeling

_____
_____

# Love Is Unselfish Benevolence

# Love Is Servanthood

## Recommended Reading

1. Morris, Leon.
   *Testaments of Love.*
   Grand Rapids: Wm. B. Eerdmans Publishing Company, 1981.

2. Jepson, J.W.
   *It All Adds Up to Love.*
   Van Nuys: Bible Voice Inc., 1977.

# Memoranda

Date this chapter was completed: _____

Signature: _____

Date this chapter was reviewed with helper: _____

Helper's Signature: _____

## Chapter Seven
# BADGE of LOVE

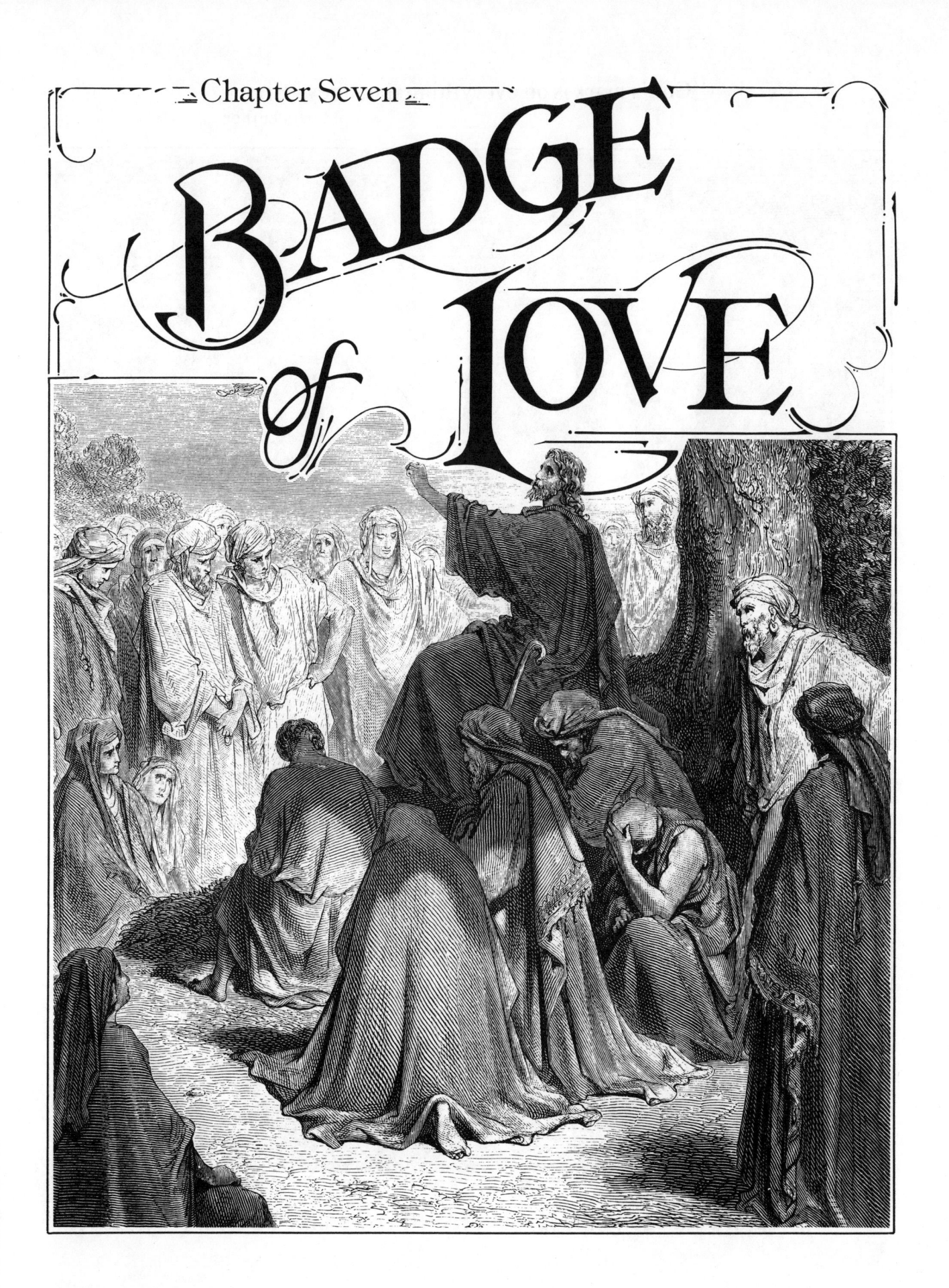

"God's mark is on everything that obeys Him."
—Martin Luther

"True knowledge of God is born out of obedience." —John Calvin

"If ye love me, keep my commandments."
(John 14:15)

"We are in bondage to the law in order that we may be free." —Cicero

# Obedience Is Loving

Jesus once stated to His disciples, "If ye love me, keep my commandments." Our love for God should be evidenced by whether we keep His commandments or not. Most of us can recall times when we would outwardly conform to a known law, but would inwardly resent the very idea of it. What if there had been no consequences for disobedience to the law? Would we have obeyed then?

O Lord, help us to really understand that your commandments are based on the principle of love and not obligation. As we learn to love you more and more, we want to let that love express itself in being obedient to your wonderful laws.

John 14:21
What are some things we know about the person who keeps God's commandments?

John 15:10
Write in your own words and personalize this verse.

## Happy to Obey

"I wish I could obey God as my little dog obeys me," said a little boy, looking thoughtfully on his shaggy friend. "He always looks so happy to obey, and I don't." What a painful truth did this child speak! Should the poor little dog readily obey his master, and we rebel against God, our Savior and the bountiful Giver of everything we love?

2 John 6
How did the writer describe love in this verse?

1 John 5:2-3
   What does God say about His commandments in these verses?

___

___

Hebrews 3:18-19
   Why did the people not enter into God's rest?

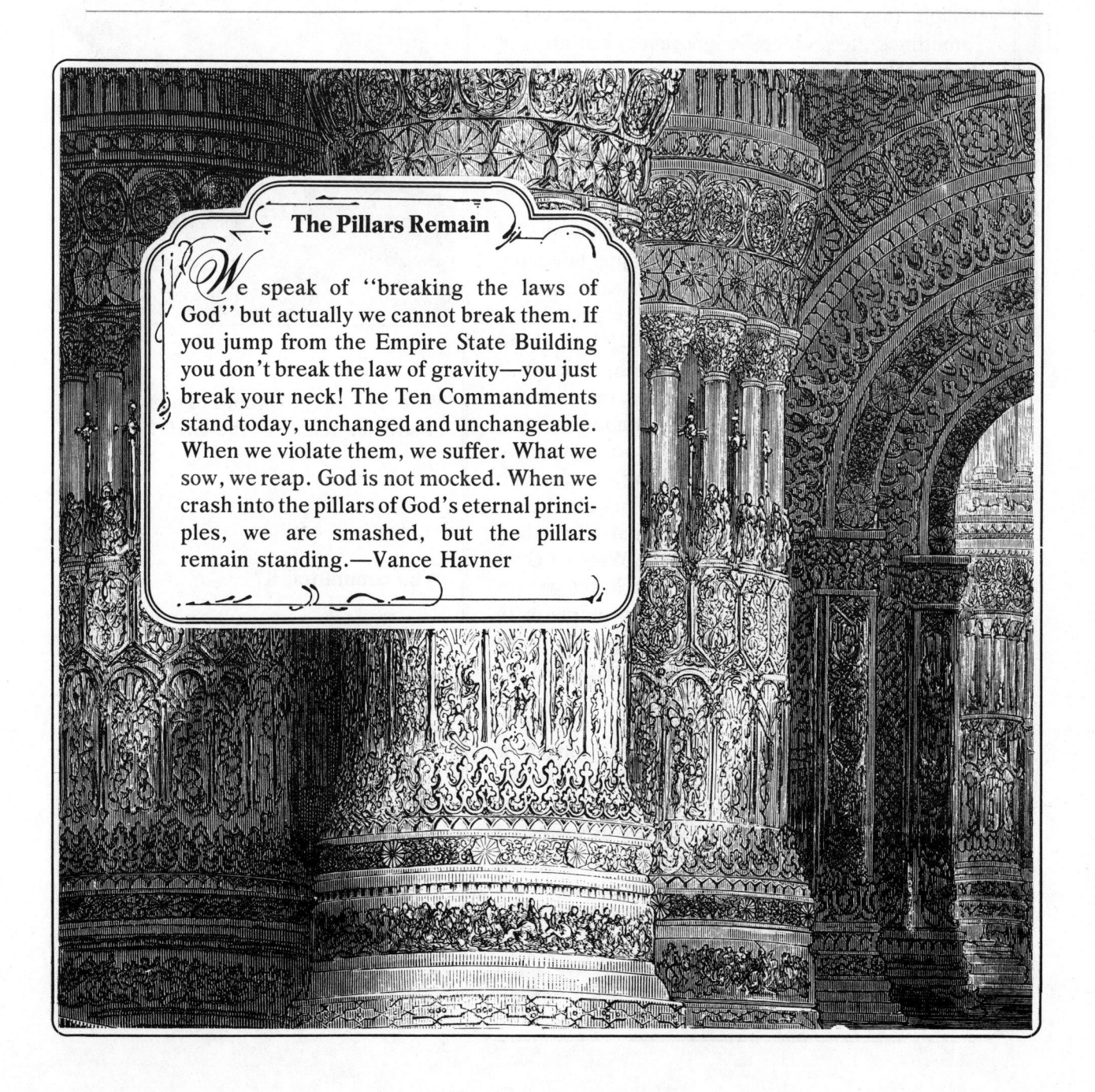

___

___

### The Pillars Remain

We speak of "breaking the laws of God" but actually we cannot break them. If you jump from the Empire State Building you don't break the law of gravity—you just break your neck! The Ten Commandments stand today, unchanged and unchangeable. When we violate them, we suffer. What we sow, we reap. God is not mocked. When we crash into the pillars of God's eternal principles, we are smashed, but the pillars remain standing.—Vance Havner

# Obedience Is Doing

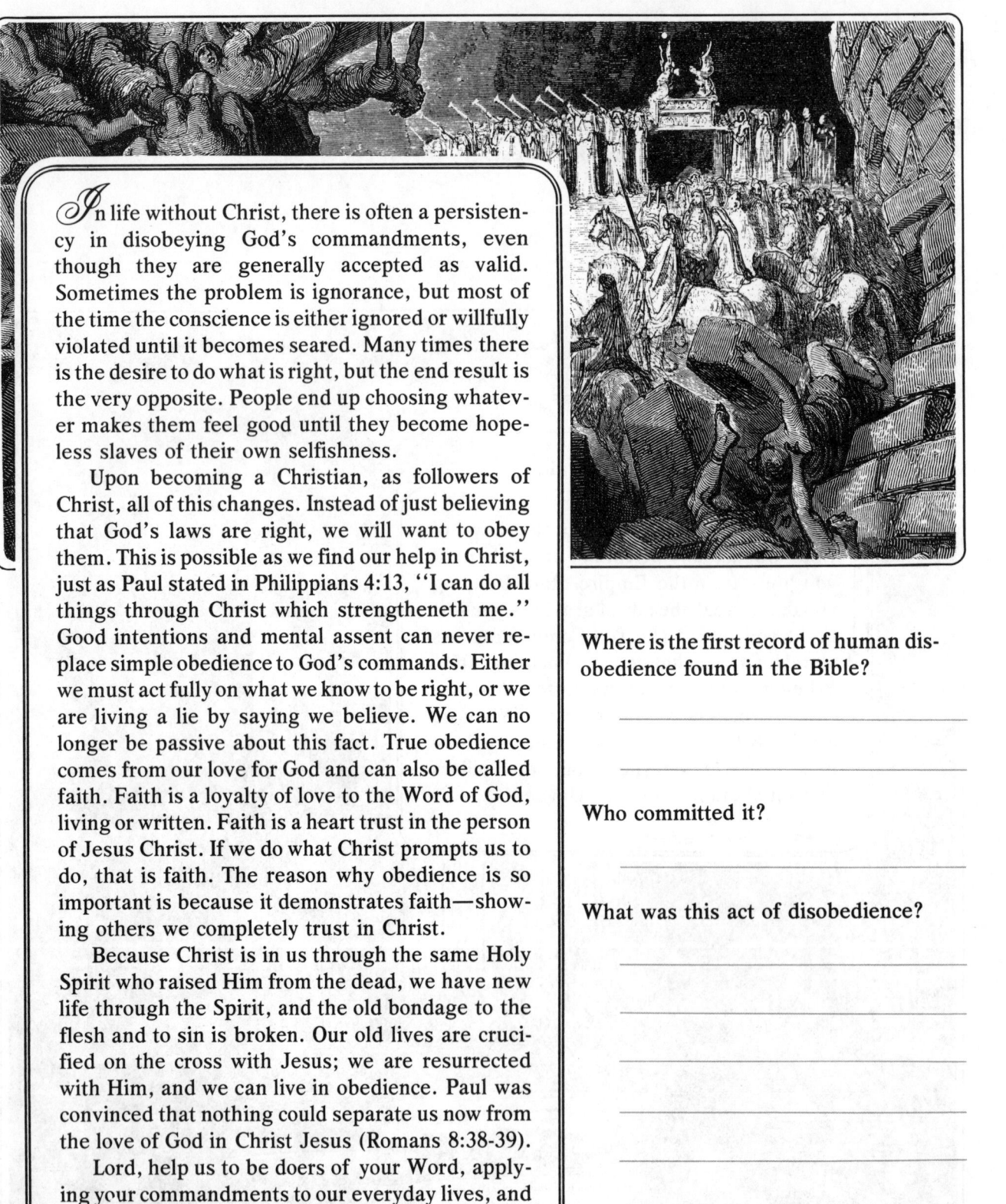

In life without Christ, there is often a persistency in disobeying God's commandments, even though they are generally accepted as valid. Sometimes the problem is ignorance, but most of the time the conscience is either ignored or willfully violated until it becomes seared. Many times there is the desire to do what is right, but the end result is the very opposite. People end up choosing whatever makes them feel good until they become hopeless slaves of their own selfishness.

Upon becoming a Christian, as followers of Christ, all of this changes. Instead of just believing that God's laws are right, we will want to obey them. This is possible as we find our help in Christ, just as Paul stated in Philippians 4:13, "I can do all things through Christ which strengtheneth me." Good intentions and mental assent can never replace simple obedience to God's commands. Either we must act fully on what we know to be right, or we are living a lie by saying we believe. We can no longer be passive about this fact. True obedience comes from our love for God and can also be called faith. Faith is a loyalty of love to the Word of God, living or written. Faith is a heart trust in the person of Jesus Christ. If we do what Christ prompts us to do, that is faith. The reason why obedience is so important is because it demonstrates faith—showing others we completely trust in Christ.

Because Christ is in us through the same Holy Spirit who raised Him from the dead, we have new life through the Spirit, and the old bondage to the flesh and to sin is broken. Our old lives are crucified on the cross with Jesus; we are resurrected with Him, and we can live in obedience. Paul was convinced that nothing could separate us now from the love of God in Christ Jesus (Romans 8:38-39).

Lord, help us to be doers of your Word, applying your commandments to our everyday lives, and so bringing glory and honor to your great name.

Where is the first record of human disobedience found in the Bible?

Who committed it?

What was this act of disobedience?

Explain in your own words what the writer is saying in James 1:22-25.

What does Jesus mean in Matthew 7:21?

Luke 6:46-48
   Explain what Jesus is saying about the person who not only hears His word but obeys it.

Luke 6:49
   What about the person who disobeys?

If faith means "to believe on" and works means "obedience to," explain James 2:17-20.

In 1 John 2:3-6, what is the proof of knowing God?

> Be good, get good, and do good. Do all the good you can; to all the people you can; in all the ways you can; as often as you can; and as long as you can.—Spurgeon

# Obedience Is Complete

As a Christian, you have within you the same Holy Spirit that Jesus had within Him, and can begin to understand that you are capable of loving obedience to God.

Even though you have been reluctant to obey in the past, have been hesitant to obey completely or have been just plain slow to obey, remember you are now a new person in Christ. Even though obedience was once a matter of convenience or compulsion for you, or you even thought it impossible, Christ's strength is now made perfect in your weakness. It doesn't matter if you failed to obey before with all your heart, soul, mind and strength, because Jesus is now Lord of your heart and obedience comes from love.

The beauty of loving and complete obedience is best seen in the life of Jesus. The Scriptures teach that He humbled Himself from the very beginning and always sought to "do" the will of the Father. His obedience was complete in every way—even to the laying down of His life. There is no better model for us to learn from than the Jesus who taught His disciples to pray, "Thy kingdom come. Thy will be done in earth, as it is in heaven"; the Jesus who told the Jews, "For I came down from heaven, not to do mine own will, but the will of him that sent me"; the Jesus who prayed in the Garden of Gethsemane, "Father, if thou be willing, remove this cup from me: nevertheless not my will, but thine be done."

Complete obedience is essential to a godly life, and is made possible by the Holy Spirit who dwelt in Christ and is now in us.
(Here's a prayer you may want to pray:)

Oh, Lord, I'm truly excited about obeying your will, because for the first time I can see that Jesus prepared the way before me by setting the perfect example of obedience. I thank and praise you for the Holy Spirit who lives inside me, teaching me how to follow Jesus, the Way, the Truth and the Life. It is my heart's desire to be totally obedient to you, no matter what the cost; and your Word promises to give me my heart's desire. I ask this in Jesus' name. Amen.

1 Samuel 12:14-15
   a) What conditions did the prophet Samuel lay out before King Saul and the people of Israel to **insure** blessing?

   _____
   _____
   _____
   _____

   b) What was the blessing if they obeyed?

   _____
   _____

## Obedience Unto Death

I remember reading in some ninth century history of a young general who with five hundred men came up against a king with twenty thousand. And the king sent a messenger to him to say that it was the height of folly to resist with his handful of men. The general called in one of his men and said, "Take that sword and drive it to your heart." And the man took the weapon, and drove it to his heart, and fell dead. He said to another, "Go jump off that cliff," and the man instantly obeyed, plunging to his death. Then, turning to the messenger, he said, "Go back and tell your king that we have five hundred such men. We will die but we will never surrender." The messenger returned, and his tale struck such terror into the hearts of the king's soldiers, so that they fled like chaff before the wind. God says, "One shall chase a thousand, and two put ten thousand to flight."

—Moody

1 Samuel 12:15
   What was the curse if they disobeyed?

1 Samuel 15:16-19
   a) Why did Saul get in trouble?

   b) How does this verse relate to each one of us?

1 Samuel 15:23
   To what did God compare the sin of rebellion or disobedience?

John 6:38
   Why did Jesus say He came down from heaven?

Philippians 2:8
   How obedient was Jesus?

# Obedience Brings Many Blessings

One of the most exciting aspects of obeying God's laws is seeing the wonderful results that follow. From the smallest child to the oldest adult, the keeping of God's commandments brings great blessings and lasting rewards.

The rewards of obedience are strong proof that God's laws were meant for our own good. Not only will your life be fulfilled each day, but you'll find that others will benefit as well. Through the wisdom and knowledge that we gain by keeping His commandments, we are able to show others what God is like. The Bible tells us that this brings great joy to His heart.

**Deuteronomy 11:26-28**
"Behold, I set before you this day a blessing and a curse; A blessing, if ye obey the commandments of the Lord your God, which I command you this day: And a curse, if ye will not obey the commandments of the Lord your God, but turn aside out of the way which I command you this day, to go after other gods, which ye have not known."

List the consequences of either obeying or disobeying in the following verses. Circle each verse after it is completed.

| Deuteronomy 6:24 | Proverbs 19:16 | Acts 5:32 | 1 Peter 1:22 |
| Deuteronomy 11:22-25 | Isaiah 1:19-20 | Colossians 3:5-6 | 1 Peter 2:7-8 |
| Psalm 25:10 | Jeremiah 7:23 | Hebrews 3:18-19 | 1 John 3:22 |
| Psalm 103:17-18 | Matthew 19:17 | Hebrews 5:9 | 1 John 3:24 |

## Curses

## Blessings

## Father Knows Best

Dr. Arnot, one of the greatest Scottish ministers, was in this country before he died. His mother died when he was only three weeks old, and there was a large family of Arnots. I suppose they missed the tenderness and love of their mother. They got the impression that their father was very stern and rigid, and that he had a great many laws and rules.

One rule was that the children should never climb trees. When the neighbors found out that the Arnot children could not climb trees, they began to tell them about the wonderful things they could see from the tops of the trees. Well, tell a boy of twelve years that he can't climb a tree, and he will get up that tree some way. And so the Arnot children were all the time teasing their father to let them climb the tree; but the old sire said:

"No."

One day he was busy reading his paper, and the boys said:

"Father is reading his paper. Let's slip down into the lot and climb a tree."

One of the little fellows stood on the top of the fence to see that father did not catch them. When his brother got up on the first branch, he said:

"What do you see?"

"Why! I don't see anything."

"Then go higher; you're not high enough."

So he went up higher, and again the little boy asked:

"Well, what do you see now?"

"I don't see anything."

"You aren't high enough; go higher."

And the little fellow went up as high as he could go, but he slipped. Down he came, and broke his leg. His brother tried to get him into the house, but he couldn't do it. He had to tell his father all about it. He said he was scared nearly out of his wits. He thought his father would be very angry. But his father just threw aside the paper, and started for the lot. When he got there, he picked the boy up in his arms, and brought him up to the house. Then he sent for the doctor. And now the boys got a new view of their father. They found out the reason why he was so stern. They said the moment the little brother got hurt, no mother could have been more loving and gentle.

My dear friends, there is not one commandment that has been given us which has not been for our highest and best interest. There isn't a commandment that hasn't come from the loving heart of God. What He wants is for us to give up that which is going to mar our happiness in this life, and in the life to come.

## List Some of Those to Whom We Should Be Obedient

1. Deuteronomy 27:10 _____
2. Colossians 3:20 _____
3. Proverbs 13:1 _____
4. Hebrews 13:17 _____

## List Some of the Commands of God in the New Testament

Scripture | Commandment
1. JOHN 15:12 — ..That ye love one another, as I have loved you
2.
3.
4.
5.
6.
7.
8.

# Memorize

John 14:15

# Review From Memory

1 John 1:8-9

Romans 12:5

Proverbs 30:5

1 Thessalonians 5:16-18

John 17:3

John 3:16

1 Corinthians 16:14

# Personal Prayer

*Heavenly Father, as I realize the importance of obedience in my life, I wish now to state before you my commitment to obey you. Humbly, on my knees I will pray and include the principles I am learning. In Jesus' name I pray.*

## Thankfulness for God's Law and Commandments

## Obedience Is Doing

## Obedience Is Loving

# Obedience Is Complete

## Obedience Brings Many Blessings

# Recommended Reading

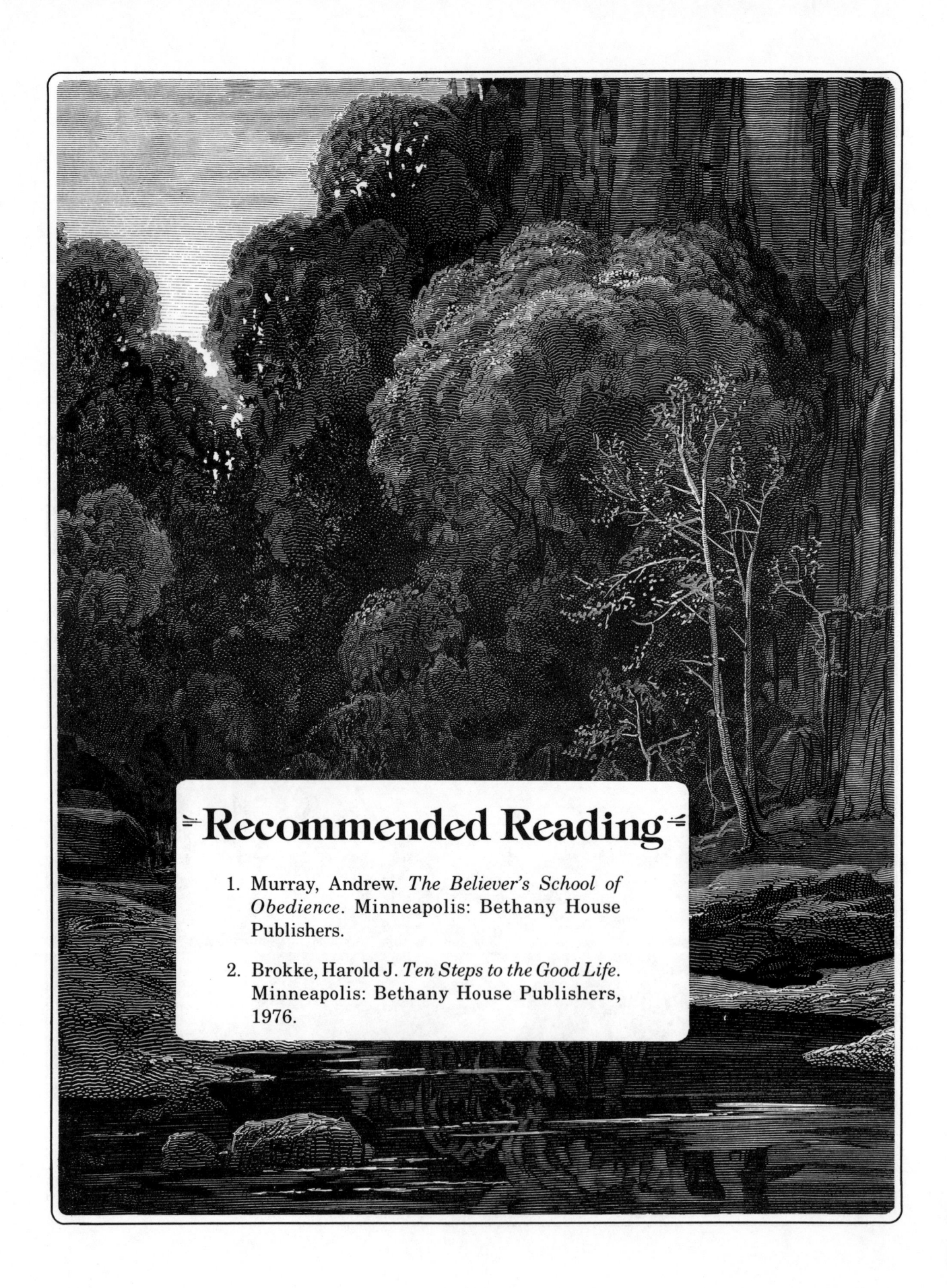

1. Murray, Andrew. *The Believer's School of Obedience*. Minneapolis: Bethany House Publishers.

2. Brokke, Harold J. *Ten Steps to the Good Life*. Minneapolis: Bethany House Publishers, 1976.

# Memoranda

Date this chapter was completed: _____

Signature: _____

Date this chapter was reviewed with helper: _____

Helper's Signature: _____

# Chapter Eight
# Testing of your Faith

"... the soul in which God works His grace, if it walks in humility and fear, it may be led into whatsoever temptation and thrown in whatsoever company, and it will gain new strength there, and win new victories and spoils there." —Santa Teresa

"Temptation is the fire that brings up the scum of the heart."
—Thomas Boston

"My brethren, count it all joy when ye fall into divers temptations; Knowing this, that the trying of your faith worketh patience. But let patience have her perfect work, that ye may be perfect and entire, wanting nothing." (James 1:2-4)

# Temptation

"Show it a fine pair of heels and run for it."

—Shakespeare

# Temptation Is Not Sin

Now that you have become a Christian you are much more sensitive to the struggle with temptation. Part of this battle is misunderstanding what temptation actually is. Through prayer and study of God's Word you will recognize scriptural insights that will help you to live an overcoming life.

Temptation is in one way an enticement, an appeal to the old way of living. In another sense it is a solicitation to do evil and a testing of your commitment to the Lord Jesus Christ. It can appear in the form of an influence, bribe, inducement, attraction, seduction, persuasion or allurement. Temptation is many things, but it is not sin. These two are often confused and consequently difficulties arise.

Temptation is like a "sales pitch," while sin is the actual purchase. The product does not have to be bought no matter how tempting it may appear. With God's help attention can be given to only those things which will draw us closer to Him.

Genesis 3:1-6 is the first recorded account of temptation in the Scriptures. Describe how Satan tempted Adam and Eve into disobeying God and bringing sin into the world.

_____

_____

_____

James 1:14-15
   a) How does this passage show that temptation is not sin?

_____

_____

b) What are the steps that lead to death?

James 1:2,3. Give the biblical definition of temptation.

### A Stronger Lion

If that roaring lion that goes about continually seeking whom he may devour finds us alone among the vineyards of the Philistines, where is our hope? Not in our heels, for he is swifter than we; not in our weapons, for we are naturally unarmed; not in our hands, which are weak and languishing; but in the Spirit of God, by whom we can do all things. If God fights in us, who can resist us? There is a stronger lion in us than against us.—Spurgeon

# Temptation Wears Many Disguises

In studying the life of Christ, it can be seen that He was tempted in a number of ways. Sometimes the temptation is obvious, at other times very subtle. The devil has the unique ability to make sin appear as something attractive and profitable. He tried with Jesus Christ, although He saw through the masquerade and exposed it for what it really was. You will be tempted like Christ, and you too must see through the disguises. Many times temptation comes with a strong appeal that looks good for the moment but which if fulfilled will later bring tragic consequences.

The Bible calls Satan "the Tempter" and we must remember that he is violently opposed to God and His Kingdom. The devil wants your allegiance, and will do anything in his power to try to destroy God's purposes both in heaven and on earth. Satan is the master of disguises and his continual intention will be to get you to turn your back on Jesus Christ.

You must be keenly aware that although God will allow you to be tested, He will never tempt you to sin. We are assured that no matter how subtle the temptation may be, it does not come from God and will never bring us closer to Him if we yield to it. His desire is that you walk in all His ways, and He will not only alert you to all temptation, but will continually help you in overcoming it.

### The One-Eyed Doe

There is an old fable that a doe who had but one eye used to graze near the sea. In order to be safe, she kept her blind eye toward the water, from which side she expected no danger, while with the good eye she watched the country. Some men, noticing this, took a boat and came upon her from the sea and shot her. With her dying breath she said,

"Oh! Hard fate! That I should receive my death wound from that side which I expected no harm, and be safe in the part where I looked for most danger."

Look up the Scriptures below and list the different titles and disguises of Satan.

Genesis 3:1-7 _____
Job 41:34 _____
Psalm 91:3 _____
Ezekiel 28:11-17 _____
Matthew 12:24 _____
Matthew 13:4,19 _____
John 10:10 _____
John 10:12 _____
John 12:31 _____
2 Corinthians 4:4 _____
1 Peter 5:8 _____
Revelation 12:10 _____
Revelation 12:9 _____

Followers of the devil can also tempt you. In 2 Corinthians 11:13-15, what are these followers called?

_____

1 John 2:16
   This passage shows that temptation works through the lust of the flesh, the lust of the eyes and the pride of life. Explain in your own words what each of these are:

(Lust of the flesh) _____
_____

(Lust of the eyes) _____
_____

(Pride of life) _____
_____

James 1:12
   How can we be certain God will not tempt us to do evil?
_____
_____

Matthew 24:24
   Why will many people in the last days be fooled by false Christs and false prophets?
_____
_____

Ephesians 4:27
   What is a safeguard against temptation?
_____

### On Satan's Ground

There is a legend that the apostle John was much distressed over the fall of a young convert. He summoned Satan before him, and reproached him for ruining so good a youth.

"I found your good youth on my ground," said Satan; "so I took him."

The only safe course is to avoid temptation altogether.

# Temptation Can Be Overcome

The dangers of yielding to temptation and the tragic consequences should convince us more than ever that we must overcome it in every area of our lives. Besides understanding what temptation is and how it operates, definite positive steps must be taken towards confronting it effectively. One weapon that Jesus used to resist temptation was the Word of God. He used it in times of great need because He knew that nothing was more powerful than the Truth. When God's Word is hidden in your heart it will serve as a safeguard against any temptation that may come. During times of great trial Christ would abstain from food, sleep or other necessities of life in order to spend much time in prayer. This gave Him victory over His flesh, clearer discernment of the enticements of the devil and the world, and great strength from the Holy Spirit in times of need.

Another principle in overcoming temptation is the power of running. "Flee temptation before it sinks its claws deep within your affections!" For example, the Bible shows us the tremendous victory Joseph had in running from a strong temptation to sin, and the tragic results that David experienced because he failed to do the same.

You must learn to be sensitive to the initial promptings of the Holy Spirit in different situations in your life. He will be faithful to show you danger if you are careful to watch and listen. Because Jesus gave an example to follow and principles to live by, you too can be an overcomer.

Matthew 4:2-3
   a) In what way did the devil first tempt Jesus? _____
   _____

   b) Why? _____
   _____

   c) What does this show you about the way in which the devil tempts? ____
   _____

Matthew 4:4
   a) How did Jesus respond to this temptation? _____
   _____

   b) What Old Testament passage was He quoting from? _____

   c) What do you think Jesus meant by His answer? _____
   _____
   _____

Matthew 4:6
   a) In His second attempt, what method did Satan use to tempt Jesus? ____
   _____
   _____

   b) What was he trying to get Jesus to do? _____
   _____

Matthew 4:7
   a) How did Jesus respond to this temptation? _____
   _____

196

b) What Old Testament passage was He quoting? _____

c) What do you think Jesus meant by His answer? _____
_____

Matthew 4:8-9
   a) The devil tries the third time. In what way is he tempting Christ this time?
_____

   b) What did he want from Jesus? _____
_____

   c) What did he offer to give Jesus? _____
_____

Matthew 4:10
   a) How did Jesus respond to this temptation? _____
_____
_____

   b) What Old Testament passage was he quoting? _____
_____

   c) What do you think Jesus meant by this? _____
_____

Matthew 4:11
   a) What two things happened to Jesus because He resisted temptation? _____
_____

   b) What can you learn from Jesus' example about temptation in your life? _____
_____

## He Silenced the Devil

If you find yourself being tempted, do like a wealthy farmer in New York State. He was once very stingy, but he became converted. Not too long after that a poor man who had been burned out and had no provisions came to him for help. The farmer thought he would be liberal and give the man a ham from his smoke-house. On his way to get it, the tempter whispered to him:

"Give him the smallest one you have."

He had a struggle whether he would give a large or a small ham, but finally he took down the largest he could find.

"You are a fool," the devil said.

"If you don't keep still," the farmer replied, "I will give him every ham I have in the smoke-house."

Hebrews 4:15-16
   Why should we look to Christ when we are tempted? _____
   _____

Matthew 26:41
   a) In the hour of trial what was Christ's commandment to His disciples? _____
   _____

   b) What do you think Christ meant by "the spirit is willing but the flesh is weak"?
   _____

Genesis 39:7-12; 2 Samuel 11:2-4
   Read these two passages and show the difference between Joseph's and David's responses.
   _____

Proverbs 4:14-15
   Rewrite these verses in your own words and personalize them. _____
   _____

Job 31:1
   How did Job protect himself from falling into temptation?

1 Peter 5:8-10
   What are some ways I can resist temptation?
   _____

1 John 4:4
   How do I know I can overcome temptation?
   _____

# Temptation Will Prove Character

Temptation should not always be viewed in a negative sense. Martin Luther, the great reformer, said it is one of three things needed for a saint's development. Temptation should not be considered only in light of the present battle but also in the glory that comes to God as He sees His children resisting it as they mature into spiritual adulthood. Every single temptation can be an opportunity for us to prove to God that we love Him supremely.

There is an old saying that goes, "The Holy One, blessed be His name, does not elevate a man to dignity until He has first tried and searched him. If this man stands in temptation, then God raises him to dignity." God does not allow temptation in order to make us sin. It is allowed to enable us to conquer sin. God has promised us we would never be tempted above our ability to overcome, and so greater temptation can establish greater character in our lives.
(Here is a suggested prayer:)

Dear Lord, I will not purposely place myself in a situation that will tempt me. As I am on the alert, applying the principles of prayer, standing on your Word and fleeing temptation, my love for you will deepen and the enemy will be defeated.

1 Corinthians 10:13
Why shouldn't we be afraid of temptation?

James 1:2-4, 12
   If I respond correctly to temptation, what will be the results?

   _____

   _____

   _____


1 Peter 1:6-7
   What good can come from temptation?

   _____

   _____


Matthew 6:13
   Should we invite temptation into our lives? _____

### Scars of Honor

Far nobler the sword that is nicked and worn,
Far fairer the flag that is grimy and torn,
Than when to the battle fresh they were borne.

He was tried and found true; He stood the test;
'Neath whirlwinds of doubt, when all the rest
Crouched down and submitted, He fought best.

There are wounds on His breast that can never be healed,
There are gashes that bleed and may not be sealed,
But, wounded and gashed, He won the field.

And others may dream in their easy chairs,
And point their white hands to the scars He bears;
But the palm and the laurel are His—not theirs!

—Anonymous

# Exercise

## Evaluate Your Areas of Greatest Temptation

𝒰sing the principles I have learned from the Scriptures, I will lift up to God the following prayer specifically involving the areas of temptation I have listed on the **previous page**.

# Memorize

1 Corinthians 10:13

James 4:7

# Review From Memory

1 John 1:8-9

Romans 12:5

Proverbs 30:5

1 Thessalonians 5:16-18

John 17:3

John 3:16

1 Corinthians 16:14

John 14:15

# Further Insights Into Understanding Temptation

Throughout the Scriptures there are many cautions from the Lord to be on the alert so we are not deceived and fall into sin. Here are some things to watch out for in the area of temptation.

## Beware:

1. Temptation may come after your greatest moments of victory.
2. Temptation may come with a question.
3. Temptation may come if you are spiritually minded.
4. Temptation may come in your weakest area.
5. Temptation may come in your greatest strengths.
6. Temptation may come if you are in a position of influence or example.
7. Temptation may come when you least expect it.
8. Temptation may come from unexpected sources.
9. Temptation may come often in the same area.
10. Temptation may withdraw for a season only to return again.

### Better Than Gold

The trial of faith is like the testing of gold in a furnace, but with one important difference—gold, though the purest of metals, is not increased in the furnace; but faith, being tried, "groweth exceedingly."

—Bowes

# Personal Prayer

*As* I learn these valuable principles on understanding and overcoming temptation, I have great confidence that God will help me to apply them and gain victory after victory for His glory. This is my prayer of gratitude to God for His continual strength in the hour of trial.

# Recommended Reading

1. Durham, Charles. *Temptation.* Downers Grove, Illinios: InterVarsity Press, 1973.

2. Lewis, C.S. *The Screwtape Letters.* Old Tappan, New Jersey: Fleming H. Revell, 1979.

# Memoranda

Date this chapter was completed: _____

Signature: _____

Date this chapter was reviewed with helper: _____

Helper's Signature: _____

## Chapter Nine
# Sharing My New Life

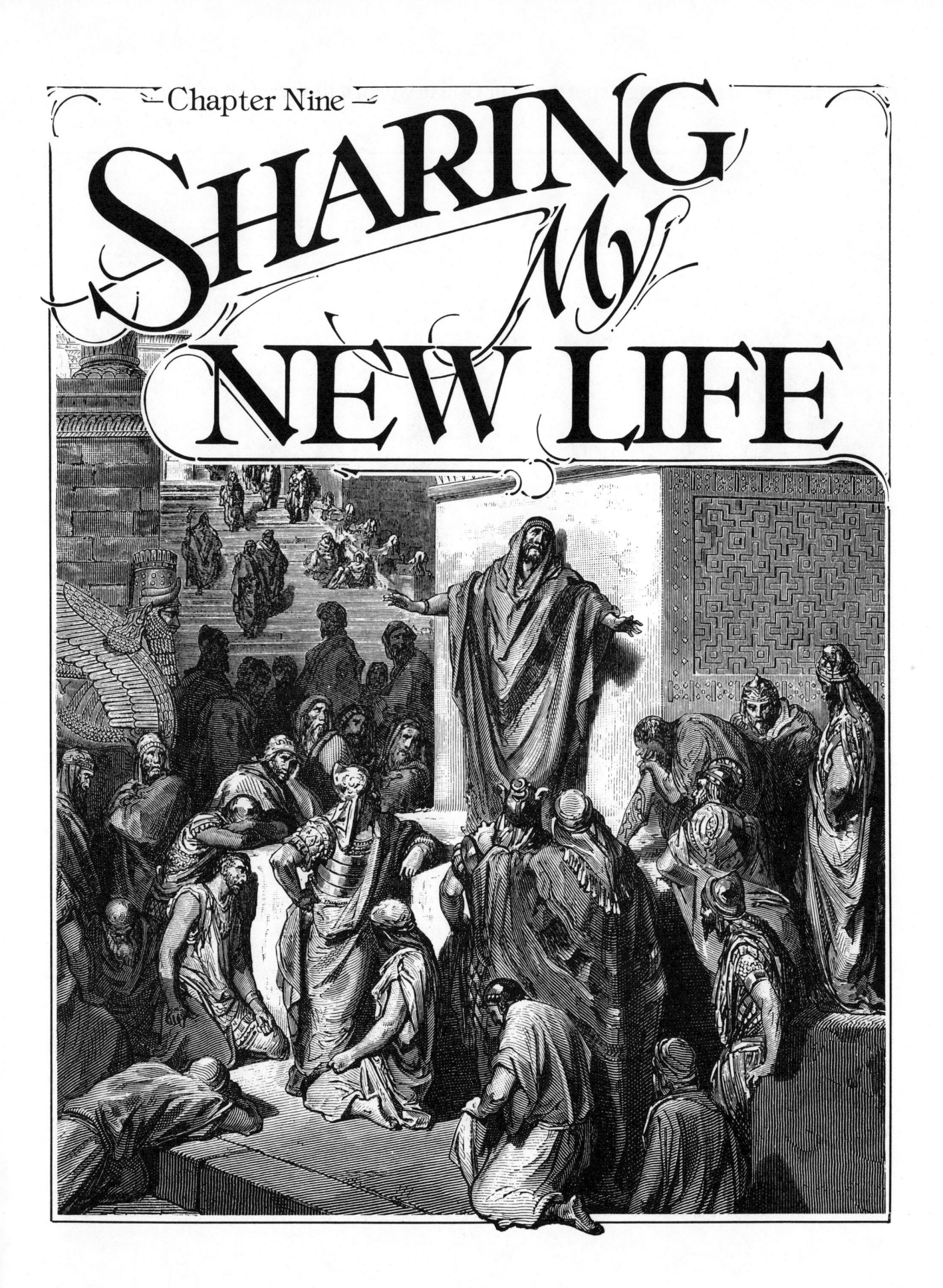

"One man with a glowing experience of God is worth a library full of arguments."
—Vance Havner

"But sanctify the Lord God in your hearts: and be ready always to give an answer to every man that asketh you a reason of the hope that is in you with meekness and fear." (1 Peter 3:15)

"...God will give you some souls, and as soon as ever you have won a soul, you won't care about any of the other things."
—D.L. Moody

"Brightness of the eternal glory, shall Thy praise unuttered lie? Who will hush the heaven-sent story of the Lamb who came to die?"
—John Bunyan

What a privilege it is to follow Jesus! Every day God's love is displayed in so many ways. To walk in Christ brings joy unspeakable, freedom from guilt, and a peace that is constant even in the most trying times. Because of this, many new believers, bold and joyful in their new-found life, rush out and tell their friends, relatives, and even strangers on the street the exciting news. Others, shy to begin with, blossom more slowly and begin sharing Christ as they learn more about Him.

"God had an only Son and He made Him a missionary."
—David Livingstone

# The Drunken Miller

I was at one time in a town in Nebraska and the people kept telling me about one man. "There is one man here, if you can get him, he is good for one hundred men for Christ."

I said, "Who is he?"

"John Champeony. He is the miller."

I said to Mr. Preston, who was then a minister, "Have you been to see him?"

"No."

I asked another minister if he had been to see the fellow, and he said no. I asked the United Presbyterian preacher (they have a college out here), and he said no, he hadn't been around to see him.

I said, "Well, I guess I'll go around to see him."

I found the fellow seated in a chair teetered back against the wall, smoking. I said, "Is this Mr. Champeony?"

"Yes, sir, that's my name." He got up and took me by the hand.

I said, "My name is Sunday; I'm down at the church preaching. A good many have been talking to me about you and I came down to see you and ask you to give your heart to God." He looked at me, walked to the cupboard, opened the door, took out a half-pint flask of whisky and threw it out on a pile of stones.

He then turned around, took me by the hand, and as the tears rolled down his cheeks he said, "I have lived in this town nineteen years, and you are the first man that has ever asked me to be a Christian."

He said, "They point their fingers at me and call me an old drunkard. They don't want my wife around with their wives because her husband is a drunkard. Their children won't play with our babies. They go by my house to Sunday school and church, but they never ask us to go. They pass us by. I never go near the church. I am a member of the lodge. I am a Mason. I went to the church eleven years ago when a member of the lodge died, but I've never been back and I said I never would go."

I said, "You don't want to treat the church that way. God isn't to blame, is He?"

"No".

"The church isn't to blame, is it?"

"No."

"Christ isn't to blame?"

"No."

"You wouldn't think much of me if I would walk up and slap your wife because you kept a dog I didn't like, would you? Then don't slap God in the face because there are some hypocrites in the church that you don't like and who are treating you badly. Come up and hear me preach, will you, John?"

"Yes, I'll come tonight."

I said, "All right, the Lord bless you, and I will pray for you." He came; the seats were all filled and they crowded him down the side aisle. I can see him now, standing there with his hat in his hand, leaning against the wall looking at me. He never took his eyes off me. When I got through and gave the invitation, he never waited for them to let him out. He walked over the back of the seats and took his stand for Jesus Christ. In less than a week seventy-eight men followed him into the kingdom of God. They elected that man chairman of the civic federation and he cleaned the town up for Jesus Christ. He has led the hosts of righteousness from then until now. Men do care to talk about Jesus Christ and about their souls. "No man cares for my soul." That's what's the trouble. They are anxious and waiting for someone to come.

—Billy Sunday

# The Power of My Testimony

As a new believer, your initial witness is the simple truth about what Jesus has done in your life. Because you know God has rescued you, freed you from past sins forever, set you in a safe place; because you have felt God's love, joy and peace; because you have experienced God's care for you; because you know He speaks and you have heard His voice in your heart; it will be almost impossible not to tell others around you that He will do the same for them.

The great thing is that no one, no matter how hard they try, can argue or explain away what you have experienced in Christ. Many will be interested, even fascinated in your life-changing story, so you can be confident in what you say, relax and let the Holy Spirit do the work in those with whom you are sharing. You must never underestimate the power of your personal testimony to lead others to Jesus.

## A Life Message

One day a minister had a man in his congregation who was not a Christian. He was an intelligent man and a lawyer. The minister wanted the man to join the church. So he organized a series of sermons to convert the lawyer. He preached on them for an entire winter, and when the services were all over, the man came to him and said, "Pastor, I want to join the church."

"Thank the Lord," said the minister "Which sermon did it?"

"None of them at all. The sermons never interested me."

"What in the world ever influenced you to join the church, then?" the minister asked.

"You know the widow in your church—the one who has to walk with crutches?"

"Yes," replied the minister.

"Well, she was going out of the church one morning and one of her crutches fell from her hand. I caught her just in time to save her from falling. And when I had held her up and given her her crutches again she said, "Thank you, sir. I hope you love my Jesus." Your sermons didn't do it, but that dear old widow's kind words did it."

Acts 4:13
   Why were people amazed and influenced by Peter's and John's testimonies?

2 Timothy 1:7-8
   Verse 8 instructs us not to be ashamed of the testimony of Jesus Christ. In verse 7 there are some reasons for this. What are they?

Revelation 12:11
   How does this verse say the devil will be overcome?

# The Power of My Life

One of the loudest witnesses to the truth of the gospel will be found in the way we live. It will bring far more lasting impressions than what we say no matter how knowledgeable we might be. As Christians we are continually under observation by those around us, so we must always be careful to reflect the love of Christ. By displaying the fruit of the Spirit—love, peace, joy, patience, kindness, goodness, faithfulness, gentleness, and self-control—in our everyday lives, we will bear witness to the truth of Christ and His gospel.

Now that you've given your heart to Christ, you will no longer want to conform to the values and standards of this world's system. As you have most assuredly noticed, people dramatically change upon becoming Christians. What was once considered desirable and important becomes distasteful and unnecessary. When you pray, ask Christ to help you be a witness for Him. Also ask Him to bring others around you so that you can show them by your example what He is like.

1 Timothy 1:16
What did God call the apostle Paul to be to others?

_____
_____
_____

1 Corinthians 11:1
Many think Jesus Christ was the only one who could live an exemplary life. What does Paul say about this?

_____
_____
_____

218

**Just a Little Gypsy Boy**

I knelt the night before in that little church alone. Nobody came to me, and nobody wanted me. I heard somebody say; "That is only a gypsy boy; no use to be concerned about him." But I cried out, "Lord Jesus, nobody wants me, but I am hungry for You."

Somehow or another, my boy's heart was strangely warmed and I went home to my father and said to him, "I am converted." The next morning I went out with supplies in my basket and the very first customer I had, I began to preach to her. I couldn't keep it in. I had received Jesus and had to tell others of Him.

Listen! When you know God is in you it will come out. The sun shines. The birds sing, and the joy of the Lord just bubbles over and flows out. You don't need to worry about people who are properly converted. They will preach for Christ. If they didn't speak at all, their lives would tell the story.

—Gypsy Smith

Paul had a powerful testimony because he displayed Christlike qualities in his everyday life. List some of those qualities recorded in Acts 20:18-36.

Romans 8:38-39
What are some other reasons why Paul's testimony was so powerful?

_____
_____
_____

Galatians 2:20
Why was Paul able to live a Christlike life?

_____
_____
_____

1 Corinthians 9:23,27
Why did Paul keep his life disciplined?

_____
_____

2 Corinthians 12:15; 2 Timothy 3:12
What are some difficulties that Paul says we can expect from being an example and sharing with others?

_____
_____
_____

2 Timothy 4:7
What was Paul able to say just before his death?

_____
_____

# The Power of My Commission

It is God's will that all of us be restored to a right and happy relationship with Him. Though His love is constantly rejected, He continues to diligently seek for those who are lost. God's tremendous burden should become one of our great concerns.

Nothing should keep us from the privilege of working hand in hand with Christ for the conversion of souls. No amount of sacrifice or suffering should be considered too great a cost. The Scriptures tell us that there is much rejoicing in heaven when one sinner repents. To see the great glory and honor this brings to God will make it all worthwhile. With singleness of mind and the Holy Spirit's help, we can spend the rest of our lives fulfilling this important mission.

### A Real Tragedy

At the Iroquois fire in Chicago six hundred people were burned to death. One young woman about seventeen years of age fought through the crowd, but her hair was singed from her head, her clothes were burned, her face blistered. She got on a street car to go to her home in Oak Park. She was wringing her hands and crying hysterically, and a woman said to her, "Why, you ought to be thankful you escaped with your life."

"I escaped—but I didn't save anybody; there are hundreds that died. To think that I escaped and didn't save anybody."

Genesis 6:5-6
Describe God's feeling over wickedness in the earth.

_____
_____
_____
_____

Matthew 9:36
How does God feel over the lost condition of people?

_____
_____
_____

1 Timothy 2:4
   What is one of God's great desires?

   _____

   _____


Matthew 4:19
   What does Jesus want us to become?

   _____

   _____

   _____


Matthew 28:19-20
   These two verses are often called the Great
   Commission. Please write them out below.

   _____

   _____

   _____

   _____

   _____

   _____

   _____

   _____

   _____

   _____


Mark 16:20
   Who will work with us?

   _____

   _____

# The Power of My Message

Two thousand years ago an event took place that split time in two and altered the destiny of the earth's people. This event has become the focal point of the Christian's message to the world. Because of it, we must all communicate clearly to others the powerful truth of the gospel.

In presenting this life-changing message, certain unalterable facts must be emphasized. First, that the Bible is the inspired, infallible Word of God. With this as a base and the Holy Spirit as our guide, we will receive insight into God's nature and character. We will understand the human race's rebellion against Him and the many ways He has dealt with them.

We will also be able to tell of the life, death and resurrection of His Son here on earth. Along with this we will be able to share about freedom from sin through the mercy and transforming power of Jesus Christ and tell of the tremendous blessings that follow those who live the way God intends them to live.

There are many other things we'll learn and be able to share as we continue to grow in the knowledge of God. We must purpose in our hearts never to compromise the Word of God in order to pacify people's consciences or please their selfish desires. We must be prepared to encounter strong opposition and persecution, knowing that our Savior was treated the same way.

Dear Lord, help me to be faithful to your cause.

Matthew 10:7
What was one thing Jesus instructed us to preach? _____
_____

Acts 26:20
What did Paul say our message should include? _____
_____

1 Corinthians 15:1-4
What else did Paul preach? _____
_____
_____
_____
_____

2 Timothy 4:3-4
What kind of message will the selfish person want to hear? _____
_____

225

2 Timothy 4:2,5
   How should I respond?

1 Timothy 4:12-16
   Go through each of these verses and write them in your own words. Try as much as possible to personalize them.

*Now fill out the page(s) on "My Personal Testimony."*
See REGISTRY

### A Thornless Crown

"Lord, You don't really mean that we shall preach the gospel to those men who murdered You—to those men who took Your life?"

"Yes," says the Lord. "Go and preach the gospel to those Jerusalem sinners." I can imagine Him saying, "Go and hunt up that man who put the cruel crown of thorns on My brow, and preach the Gospel to him. Tell him he shall have a crown in My kingdom without a thorn in it."

# Special Meditation

*In* Matthew 10 Jesus gave special instructions to those He sent out. Schedule a time to go through and meditate on this chapter relating these instructions to your new commission.

Matthew 10

## Exercise

*In Matthew 5:13 Jesus said we are the salt of the earth. Explain this metaphor in relation to the power of your life as a witness for Christ and His kingdom.

## Salt of the Earth

# Exercise

In Matthew 5:14-16 Jesus said we are the light of the world. Explain this metaphor in relation to the power of your life as a witness for Christ and His kingdom.

## Light of the World

# Special Project

Because I want God to be glorified, I am praying specifically for these people to find new life in Christ:

| Name | Date Prayer Started | Date Prayer Answered |
|------|---------------------|----------------------|
|      |                     |                      |

I am actively witnessing to these following people:

|  Name | Address | Phone # |
|---|---|---|

(At home)

(At work)

(At school)

(Other)

*Be sure to fill out both the "Biographical Sketch of My First Convert" and "Gone Fishing."*
See REGISTRY

# Memorize

Matthew 28:19-20

## Review From Memory

1 John 1:8-9

Romans 12:5

Proverbs 30:5

1 Thessalonians 5:16-18

John 17:3

John 3:16 _____
_____
_____

1 Corinthians 16:14 _____
_____
_____

John 14:15 _____
_____
_____

1 Corinthians 10:13 _____
_____
_____

James 4:7 _____
_____

# ~∈ Personal Prayer ⇒~

> Realizing your concern, dear Lord, over fallen humanity and understanding more fully the importance of being a witness, I purpose in my heart to be a living testimony for Christ. I will apply the different principles I am learning in order to accomplish your call on my life. Humbly, on my knees I pray.

The Power of My Testimony

The Power of My Life

The Power of My Commission

The Power of My Message

# Recommended Reading

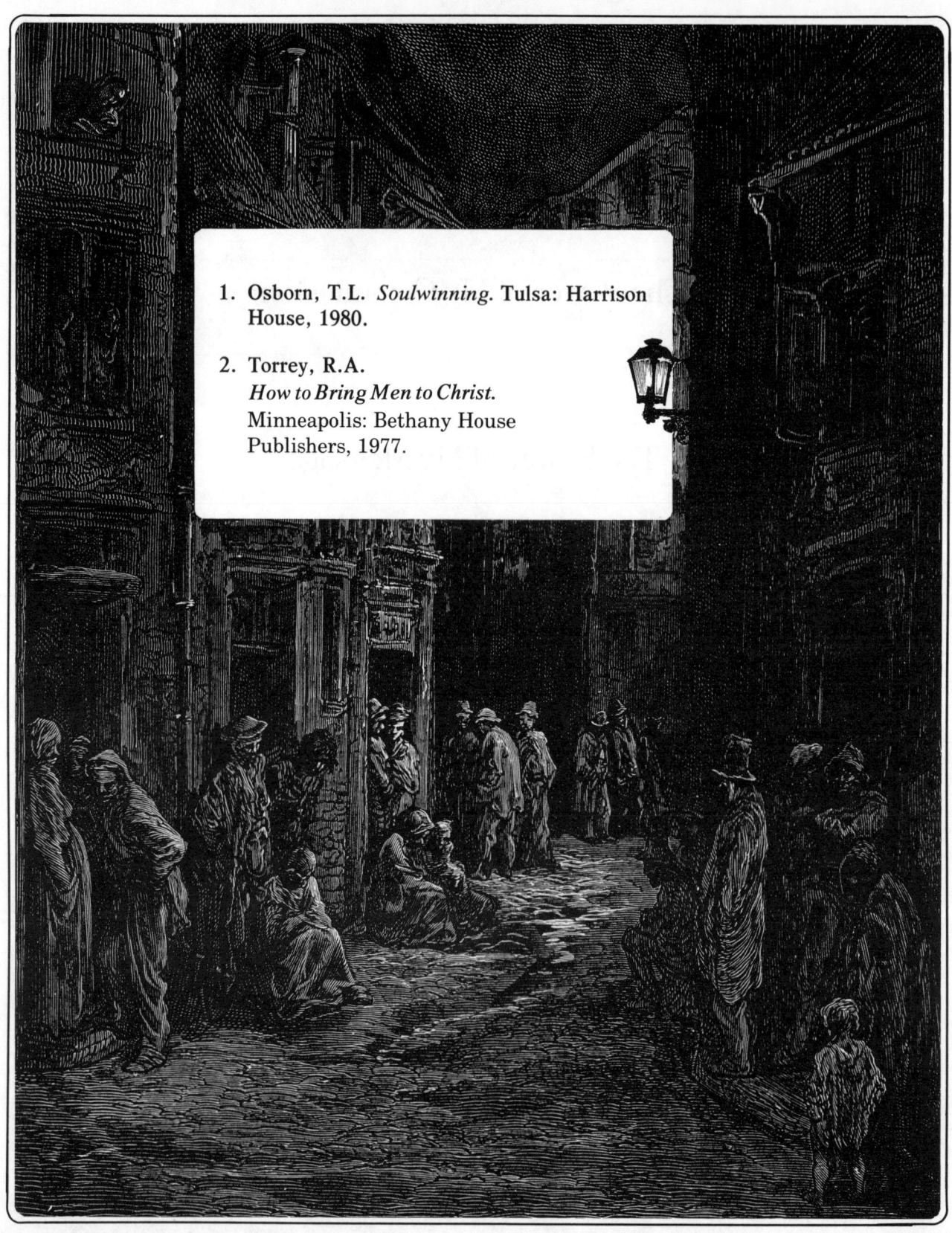

1. Osborn, T.L. *Soulwinning.* Tulsa: Harrison House, 1980.

2. Torrey, R.A. *How to Bring Men to Christ.* Minneapolis: Bethany House Publishers, 1977.

# Memoranda

Date this chapter was completed: _____

Signature: _____

Date this chapter was reviewed with helper: _____

Helper's Signature: _____

## Chaper Ten
# Power from God

Following the Lord Jesus Christ is a great privilege and blessing, but it can't be done in our own strength and wisdom. "Keep watch with Me," Jesus asked James, John and Peter in the garden at Gethsemane while He prayed over His coming ordeal. Three times they fell asleep on the crucial night of their Lord's betrayal! "The spirit indeed is willing, but the flesh is weak," He warned them.

Later, on the day of Pentecost, after their Lord's betrayal and crucifixion, a hundred and twenty disciples (including the apostles) were waiting in an upper room when a noise like a rushing wind filled the house, flickering fires fell on their heads and they were suddenly filled with the Holy Spirit. They were no longer ashamed, fearful and weak, but were powerfully transformed into dynamic, bold and victorious witnesses for Christ.

We, too, need a power beyond our own abilities to walk in the footsteps of Jesus. That power is available to us today, just as it was to the disciples of Jesus nearly 2,000 years ago.

"I maintain that the only indispensable qualification for witnessing for Christ is the Holy Ghost."
—Catherine Booth

### The Birth of the Church

On the day of Pentecost Christianity faced the world a new religion without a history, without a priesthood, without a college, without a people, and without a patron. She had only her two sacraments and her tongue of fire. The latter was her sole instrument of aggression. —William Arthur

"The very fact that we believe one thing and some of us another does not do away with the fact that God says be filled with the Holy Spirit. I believe that is the greatest need of the church of Jesus Christ today."
—Billy Graham

**"Not by might, nor by power, but by my Spirit, saith the Lord of hosts." (Zechariah 4:6)**

# The Promise of the Spirit

The promise that the Holy Spirit would come was given by the prophet Joel hundreds of years before Christ: "And it shall come to pass afterward, that I will pour out my spirit upon all flesh; and your sons and your daughters shall prophesy, your old men shall dream dreams, your young men shall see visions" (Joel 2:28). Jesus referred to this promise when He told His disciples He would send them a "helper" or "comforter" after His death, but no doubt they were puzzled by what He meant—until Pentecost!

While baptism with water was a public declaration of the early disciples' commitment to Christ, the baptism into the Holy Spirit was different. This new baptism resulted in a great increase of spiritual understanding and brought forth many different gifts that were used to most effectively reach the world with the gospel.

The baptism distinctly included the following things: the power of a holy life; the power of a self-sacrificing life; the power of a cross-bearing life; the power of great meekness; the power of a loving enthusiasm in proclaiming the gospel; the power of teaching and preaching; the power of a loving and living faith; the gift of tongues; an increase of power to work miracles; the gift of inspiration, or the revelation of truths before unrecognized by them; the power of moral courage to proclaim the gospel and do the bidding of Christ, whatever it cost them.

Matthew 3:11
Who did John say would baptize you in the Holy Spirit?

_____
_____
_____
_____

John 14:16-17
   a) What did Jesus pray for?

   b) How long would He stay?

   c) Who would He help?

   d) What would He do?

John 14:26
List some things the Holy Spirit will do.

## What Made the Difference?

A university professor was greeted by a man who took him by the hand and said, "What do you think of the Holy Spirit?" The professor answered that he regarded the Holy Spirit as an influence for good, a sort of emanation from God. The man talked to him and tried to show him his mistake. A few months later he met him again. "What do you think of the Holy Spirit now?" he asked. The professor answered, "Well, I know that the Holy Spirit is a person. Since I talked with you and have come to that conviction, I have succeeded in bringing sixty-three students to Christ."

Many things happened to the early Christians after being filled with the Holy Spirit. Match the following Scriptures with the proper displays of power listed below.

Acts 5:42    Acts 9:36-42    Acts 10:45-46    Acts 20:22-24    Acts 6:10    Acts 4:32-33    Acts 4:31

Power of:                                    Write in matching scripture reference:

a) Self-sacrificing life

b) Teaching and preaching

c) Loving, living faith

d) Tongues

e) To work miracles

f) Wisdom

g) Boldness to proclaim the gospel

# The Purpose of the Spirit

Even though the previously mentioned displays of power were essential to the early church's success, they neither separately nor all together made up completely that power which Christ promised to His followers. What they obviously received and most assuredly understood Him to have promised was the power to prevail with both God and man. This power to fix heart-searching and soul-saving conviction upon the minds of people was the highest, the most important crowning means of success in their work.

## With or Without Power

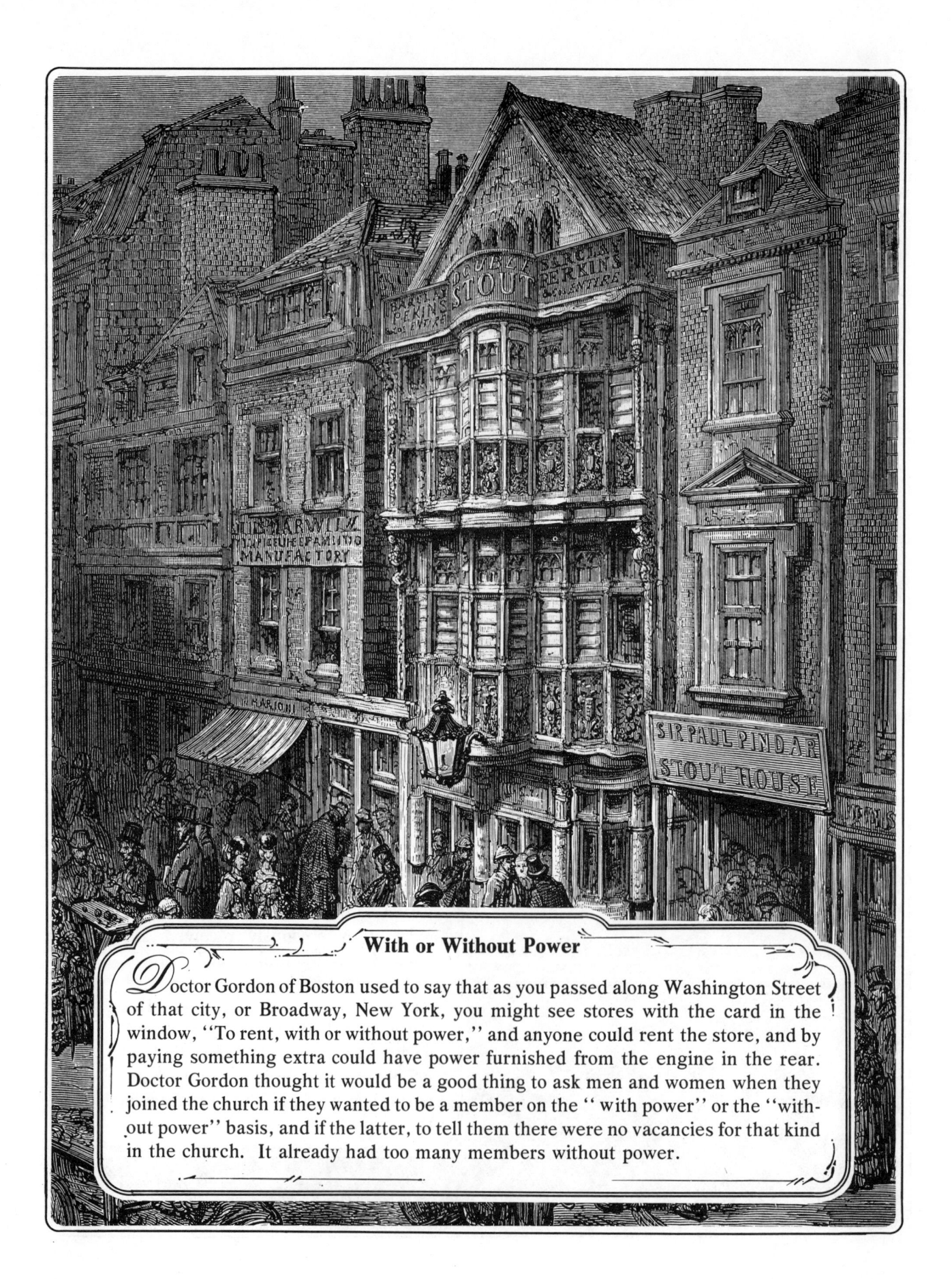

Doctor Gordon of Boston used to say that as you passed along Washington Street of that city, or Broadway, New York, you might see stores with the card in the window, "To rent, with or without power," and anyone could rent the store, and by paying something extra could have power furnished from the engine in the rear. Doctor Gordon thought it would be a good thing to ask men and women when they joined the church if they wanted to be a member on the "with power" or the "without power" basis, and if the latter, to tell them there were no vacancies for that kind in the church. It already had too many members without power.

Acts 1:8
   What was the key reason why the early Christians received the Holy Spirit?
   _____
   _____

Acts 2:37,41
   What were some of the results of Peter's preaching after he was filled with the Holy Spirit?
   _____
   _____

John 16:7,13,14
   a) Why did Jesus say He should leave?
   _____
   _____

   b) List some of the results of the Holy Spirit coming in Jesus' place.
   _____
   _____
   _____
   _____

# The Need of the Spirit

After His resurrection, Jesus appeared to His disciples and said, "Go ye therefore, and teach all nations, baptizing them in the name of the Father, and of the Son, and of the Holy Ghost: Teaching them to observe all things whatsoever I have commanded you: and, lo, I am with you alway, even unto the end of the world…" (Matthew 28:19,20).

As Christians, we have the same commission to carry out as the early disciples. And to carry out that commission we need the baptism of power in the Holy Spirit just as they did. The disciples had a promise from God. We have the same promise.

Every Christian has a measure of the Holy Spirit, enough to lead them in prayer, devotion and dedication to God. But conversion is not to be confused with empowerment to carry out the Great Commission. Conversion is a personal agreement between the sinner and Christ concerning salvation. In conversion, the soul gives up its prejudices, its antagonisms, its self-righteousness, its unbelief, its selfishness; accepts Christ, trusts Him and supremely loves Him. It appears that the disciples before Pentecost had more or less done all of this. But as yet, they had not received a definite commission and no particular provision of power to carry out this commission.

The empowerment is the promise given to those who accept the service in which Christ intends to use them. If the commission is wholeheartedly accepted and the promise is believed, if the instruction to wait upon the Lord until our strength is renewed is observed, we will receive power from on high. Therefore, we must not grieve or resist the Holy Spirit. Instead, we must accept the commission and completely devote ourselves to the saving of souls as our great and only lifework. Let's come to God with all that we have and are, and persist in prayer until we receive the promise.

It's important that all Christians should understand that this commission to convert the world is given to them individually by Christ. Everyone has the great responsibility to win as many souls as possible to Christ. This is the great privilege and duty of all His disciples. There are a great many parts in this work, but in every part we may and should have this power. Whether we preach, pray, write, do business, travel, take care of children or administer the government—whatever we do—our whole life and influence should be filled with this power. Christ says, "If any man believes, out of his belly shall flow rivers of living water." This means an impartation of power and love from the Holy Spirit to impress the truth of Christ upon the hearts of everyone.

(Adapted from *Power From on High* and *Revival Lectures,* Charles G. Finney.)

### Time for Power

Samson, with the Holy Spirit upon him, could take the jawbone of an ass and lay dead a thousand Philistines. Samson without the Holy Spirit was as weak as a newborn babe, and they poked his eyes out and cut off his locks. And so with the church and her members. Without the Holy Spirit you are as sounding brass and tinkling cymbals, simply four walls and a roof, a pipe organ and a preacher to do a little stunt on Sunday morning and evening. I tell you, Christian people, that with the Holy Spirit there is not a power on earth or in hell that can stand before the church of Jesus Christ.

The church today needs power. It has plenty of wealth, culture and numbers. There is no substitute for the Holy Spirit, and you cannot have power without the Holy Spirit. The Holy Spirit is ours by the promise of Christ. And the damnable, hell-born, whisky-soaked, hog-jowled, rum-soaked moral assassins have damned this community long enough. Now it is time it was broken up and it is time to do something.

While at Pentecost one sermon saved 3,000 people, now it takes 3,000 sermons to get one old buttermilk-eyed, whisky-soaked blasphemer.—Billy Sunday

Acts 2:39
  To whom is the promise of the Spirit given?

Why should I be filled with the Holy Spirit? Write out in your own words:

## Scripture:                                    ## Reason:

a) Luke 11:13
b) Ephesians 5:18
c) 1 Corinthians 4:20
d) 2 Timothy 1:7
e) Acts 4:31
f) Acts 4:8, 13

Write in your own words what each verse says you must do in order to receive the promise of the Spirit.

## Scripture:                        ## I will receive the promise by:

a) Acts 2:38
b) John 7:37-39
c) Acts 5:32
d) Luke 11:9-13
e) Acts 8:15-17

# Further Insights in Being Filled With the Spirit

As a Spirit-filled Christian, you will experience various testings as well as great victories in much the same way the early Christians did. Listed below are things you should expect if you are Spirit-filled.

1. You will be very useful in helping advance the kingdom of God on the earth.
2. You will be wise in winning souls.
3. People may often think you are unusual or even crazy, but only because you have different motives, views, and are influenced by a different Spirit.
4. Often you will feel a tremendous burden for the lost and the church.
5. The devil will violently oppose you.
6. Nominal church-goers and the world will oppose you.
7. You will often have great conflicts with your own flesh.
8. In the midst of all opposition, you will sense a deep peace with God.
9. You will be calm and joyful when going through hardships and trials.
10. You will always be prepared to meet the Lord Jesus face to face.

# Quotes From Several Men of God on the Subject of Being Filled With the Holy Spirit

"This power of the Spirit is meant for all who are Christians. It is a great blessing for the Presbyterian elder as well as for the preacher." —Billy Sunday

"If Christ did not permit these men, who had received so rare and unparalleled a schooling for the work to which He had so definitely and clearly called them; if He did not permit them to undertake this work without receiving, in addition, the baptism with the Holy Spirit, what is it for us to undertake the work to which He has called us until we have received the baptism with the Holy Spirit? Is it not most daring presumption?"
—R.A. Torrey

"In some sense the Holy Spirit dwells with every believer; but there is another gift, which may be called the gift of the Holy Spirit for service."
—D.L. Moody

"There were two great things we had begun to learn: that an essential experience for all true soul-winners was the anointing of the Holy Ghost, and that all effective 'revival' work must be the outcome of prayer in the Spirit."
—J.G. Govan

"This then is the great danger, namely, that outwardly the work of God can be carried on without the presence and power of the Holy Spirit, for unless He has been poured out, all that is done is in the natural and counts for nothing so far as the kingdom of God is concerned... All down the centuries those used of God have been anointed men. They have waited in God's presence until they have been endued with power from on high."
—Dr. Oswald J. Smith

"My conviction is that the Divine power, so manifest in the church at Pentecost, was nothing more nor less than what should be in evidence in the church today."
—Jonathan Goforth

"The supreme want of all missions in the present day is the manifested presence of the Holy Ghost. There has been a measure of blessing among us and souls have been saved, but where are the ones that chase a thousand, or the two that put ten thousand to flight? Where are the once-thirsty ones, now filled, from whom flow rivers of living water?"
—Hudson Taylor

## Memorize

Acts 1:8 _____
_____
_____

## Review From Memory

1 John 1:8-9 _____
_____
_____
_____

Romans 12:5 _____

Proverbs 30:5 _____
_____
_____
_____
_____
_____

1 Thessalonians 5:16-18 _____
_____
_____
_____
_____
_____
_____
_____
_____
_____
_____
_____

John 17:3

John 3:16

1 Corinthians 16:14

John 14:15

1 Corinthians 10:13

James 4:7

Matthew 28:19-20

# Prayer and Application

*L*ord Jesus, I realize I must have the power of the Holy Spirit in my life, and I ask you to fill me with that power from on high that you sent to your disciples at Pentecost. I dedicate myself entirely to the great commission of winning souls, and humbly confess my great need for the filling of the Holy Spirit to carry out this call. With all of my heart I earnestly pray the following prayer.

*You may now want to review or start your "Power from God Journal."*
See REGISTRY
*If you have completed this text book including things in the Registry, then you may want to fill out the Certificate of Completion.*
See REGISTRY

# Recommended Reading

1. Brengle, Samuel L. *When the Holy Ghost is Come.* Atlanta: The Salvation Army Supplies and Purchasing Dept., 1976.
2. Torrey, R.A. *The Baptism of the Holy Spirit.* Minneapolis: Bethany House Publishers, 1972.

# Memoranda

Date this chapter was completed: _____

Signature: _____

Date this chapter was reviewed with helper: _____

Helper's Signature: _____

# REGISTRY

Registry (rej-e-stre) n.
1. the act of recording or writing in a register. 2. a series of facts recorded. 3. an official record book or an entry in one. 4. any account entered on paper to preserve the remembrance of what is done.

**"And he appointed certain of the Levites to minister before the ark of the Lord, and to *record*, and to thank and praise the Lord God of Israel." (1 Chron. 16:4)**

It seems often that negative experiences are more easily remembered than positive ones. To counteract this, it is very helpful to write down and keep as a reminder the tremendous blessings that have come our way. By recording the great things that God has done for us, we will better remember His concern, love and faithfulness.

To keep some kind of journal and to review it occasionally will not only be a great source of inspiration but a constant reminder that "every good gift and every perfect gift is from above, and cometh down from the Father of lights." (James 1:17) The natural result of practicing this simple principle should be a heart that overflows with thanksgiving and is full of praise and worship to the King of Kings and Lord of Lords.

# Birth Certificate

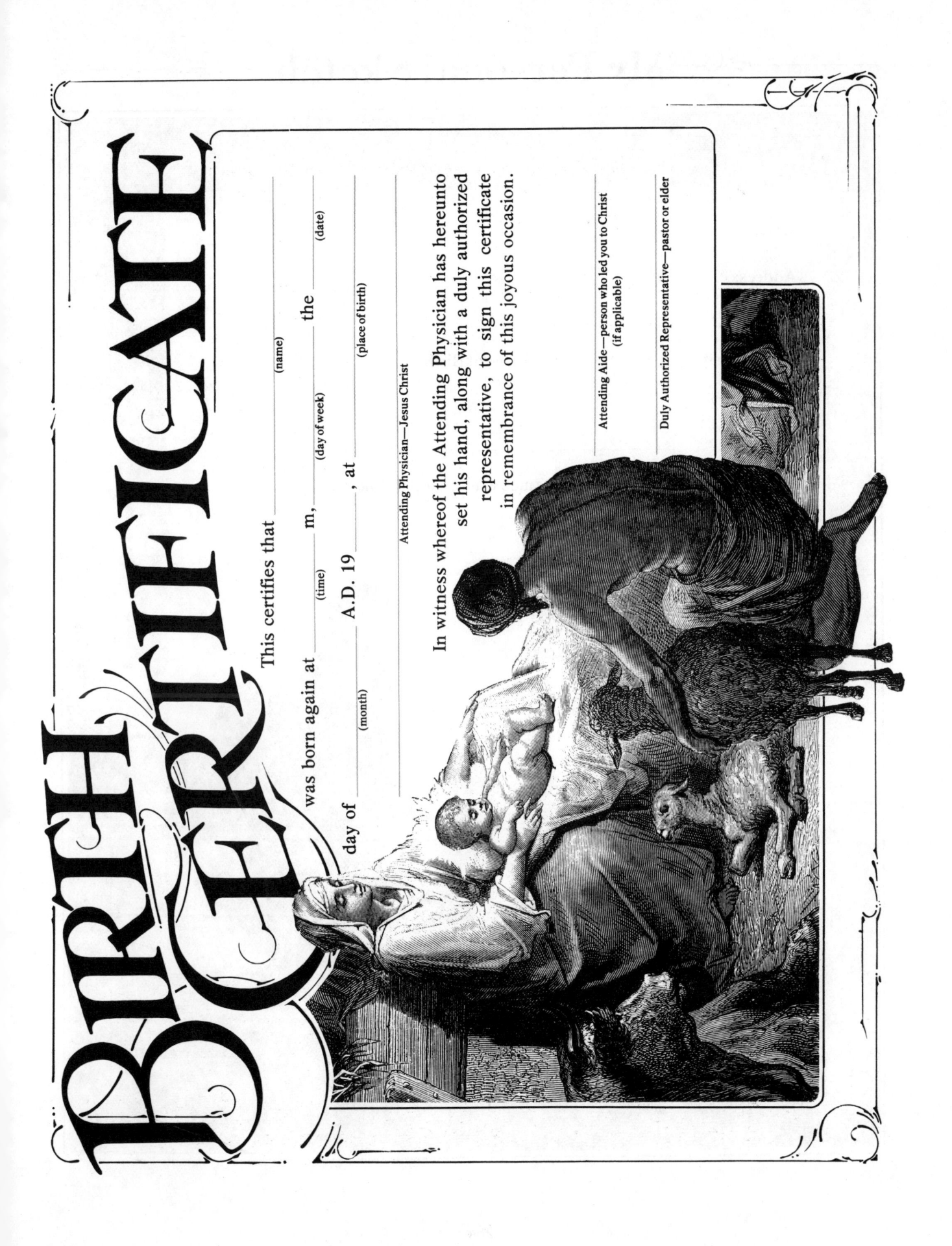

This certifies that _____
                        (name)

was born again at _____ m, _____ the _____
                   (time)    (day of week)      (date)

day of _____ A.D. 19 ____ , at _____
       (month)                         (place of birth)

_____
Attending Physician—Jesus Christ

In witness whereof the Attending Physician has hereunto set his hand, along with a duly authorized representative, to sign this certificate in remembrance of this joyous occasion.

_____
Attending Aide—person who led you to Christ
(if applicable)

_____
Duly Authorized Representative—pastor or elder

# My Personal Sketch

Name_____ Age_____

Address_____

Phone_____

Date of Birth_____ Place of Birth_____

Nationality_____

Occupation_____

My family members (Write full names wherever possible)

Father_____

Mother_____

Brothers and sisters_____

_____

_____

Spouse_____

Children_____

_____

_____

_____

_____

Most memorable person I have ever met

My religious background (if any)


The meaning of my given name is

Version of the Bible I use

My favorite Scripture  (Write out)






My favorite hymn

My favorite story in the Bible

My favorite character in the Bible

Person in the Bible I would like to pattern my life after

Why?




Some spiritual goals I would like to see accomplished in my lifetime

# I Will Always Remember

These are just some dates you may want to record. Think of others.

I was first witnessed to:      Date: _____

Comment: _____

_____

I gave my life to Christ:      Date: _____

Comment: _____

_____

I received my first answered prayer:   Date: _____

Comment: _____

_____

I received my first Bible:　　　　　　　　　Date: _____

Comment: _____

_____

I started my daily meditation in the Bible:　　Date: _____

Comment: _____

_____

I became part of a local church:　　　　　　Date: _____

Name of church: _____

Comment: _____

_____

I was baptized in water:　　　　　　　　　Date: _____

Comment: _____

_____

I witnessed to my first person:　　　　　　Date: _____

Name: _____

Comment: _____

_____

I finished the "Life in Christ" text:　　　　Date: _____

Comment: _____

_____

I led my first convert to the Lord:　　　　　Date: _____

Name: _____

Comment: _____

_____

I took my first convert through this text:　　Date: _____

Comment: _____

_____

My first Christian fast:　　　　　　　　　Date: _____

Comment: _____

_____

I finished reading my Bible completely through:　Date: _____

Comment: _____

_____

# I Will Always Remember

_____  Date: _____

Comment: _____

_____

_____  Date: _____

Comment: _____

_____

_____  Date: _____

Comment: _____

_____

_____  Date: _____

Comment: _____

_____

_____  Date: _____

Comment: _____

_____

_____  Date: _____

Comment: _____

_____

_____  Date: _____

Comment: _____

_____

_____  Date: _____

Comment: _____

_____

_____  Date: _____

Comment: _____

_____

_____  Date: _____

Comment: _____

# Certificate of Baptism

This certifies that _____

was baptized in water according to the Scripture, "Go ye therefore, and teach all nations, baptizing them in the name of the Father, and of the Son, and of the Holy Spirit." (Matt. 28:19)

on the _____ day of _____ in the _____

year of our Lord nineteen hundred and _____

_____
Pastor

# My Home Church

Name of church I am part of _____

Address of my church _____

Phone _____

My Pastor's name _____

My Pastor's address _____

Phone _____

Name of my Pastor's wife _____

**Elders or Deacon Board:**

_____
_____
_____
_____

Person I can call in case of spiritual emergency:

Name _____

Address _____

Phone _____

Others in the church that will be my spiritual supporters:

_____
_____
_____

Other members in the church I am part of: (put more than 2)

Name _____

Address _____

Phone _____


Name _____

Address _____

Phone _____


These are the different church meetings I will actively become a part of:

| Type of meeting _____ | Type of meeting _____ |
| Time of meeting _____ | Time of meeting _____ |
| Place of meeting _____ | Place of meeting _____ |

| Type of meeting _____ | Type of meeting _____ |
| Time of meeting _____ | Time of meeting _____ |
| Place of meeting _____ | Place of meeting _____ |

Here are some ways I can initially serve in my church: _____
_____

# Biographical Sketch of My "Spiritual Father"

"For though ye have ten thousand instructors in Christ, yet have ye not many fathers: for in Christ Jesus I have begotten you through the gospel." (1 Corinthians 4:15)

My "spiritual father's" name _____

My "spiritual father's" given name means _____

My "spiritual father's" address _____
_____

Phone _____  Date of Birth _____

Place of Birth _____

My "spiritual father's" nationality _____

My "spiritual father's" occupation _____

My "spiritual father's" family members (Write full names whenever possible)

Father _____  Mother _____

Brothers and sisters _____
_____
_____
_____
_____

Spouse _____

Children _____
_____
_____
_____

My "spiritual father's" religious background (if any) _____

_____

Date my "spiritual father" was born again _____

Date my "spiritual father" was baptized in water _____

Church my "spiritual father" is a part of _____

First person my "spiritual father" led to the Lord _____

_____

When _____ Where _____

Version of the Bible my "spiritual father" uses _____

_____

My "spiritual father's" favorite Scripture (Write out) _____

_____

_____

_____

Favorite hymn _____

Favorite character in the Bible _____

Favorite story in the Bible _____

Most memorable book (other than the Bible) _____

_____

Most memorable person my "spiritual father" has ever met

_____

Some spiritual goals my "spiritual father" would
like to see accomplished in his or her lifetime

_____

_____

# Biographical Sketch of the Person Helping Me Through this Text

My helper's name _____

My helper's given name means _____

My helper's address _____

Phone _____

Date of Birth _____

Place of Birth _____

My helper's nationality _____

My helper's occupation _____

My helper's family members (Write full names wherever possible)

Father _____

Mother _____

Brothers and sisters _____

_____

Spouse _____

Children _____

_____

_____

My helper's religious background (if any) _____

_____

Date my helper was born again _____

date my helper was baptized in water _____

Church my helper is a part of _____

First person my helper led to the Lord _____

_____

When _____ Where _____

Version of the Bible my helper uses _____

My helper's favorite Scripture. (Write out) _____

_____

_____

_____

Favorite hymn _____

_____

Favorite character in the Bible _____

Favorite story in the Bible _____

Most memorable book (other than the Bible) _____

Most memorable person my helper has ever met _____

_____

Some spiritual goals my helper would like to see accomplished in his or her lifetime

_____

_____

_____

# Journal of Prayer

It was George Muller's (1805-1898) custom to record his prayers and then date them when they were answered. This became a habit of his life and history tells us that he had thousands of answered prayers recorded yearly. You may want to start on this same kind of journey.

| Specific Prayer | Date First Prayed | How Prayer Was Answered | Date |
|---|---|---|---|
| | | | |

| Specific Prayer | Date First Prayed | How Prayer Was Answered | Date |
| --- | --- | --- | --- |

# My Personal Testimony

Write out your personal testimony. It should involve some of your past and present, and could involve future hopes you may have. Be careful not to exaggerate or generalize. Make it a written witness to the Christ who set you free.

_____

_____

_____

(Date) (Signature)

# Biographical Sketch of My First Convert

My convert's name _____

My convert's given name means _____

My convert's address _____
Phone _____
Date of birth _____
My convert's nationality _____
My convert's occupation _____

My convert's family members (write full names wherever possible)

Father

Mother

Brothers and sisters

Spouse

Children

Date my convert was born again

Date my convert was baptized in water

Church my convert is a part of

My convert's religious background (if any)

My convert's favorite Scripture (Write out)

Favorite hymn

Favorite character in the Bible

Favorite story in the Bible

Version of the Bible my convert uses

Some spiritual goals my convert would like to see accomplished in his or her lifetime

First person my convert led to the Lord

When                           Where

# Gone Fishing

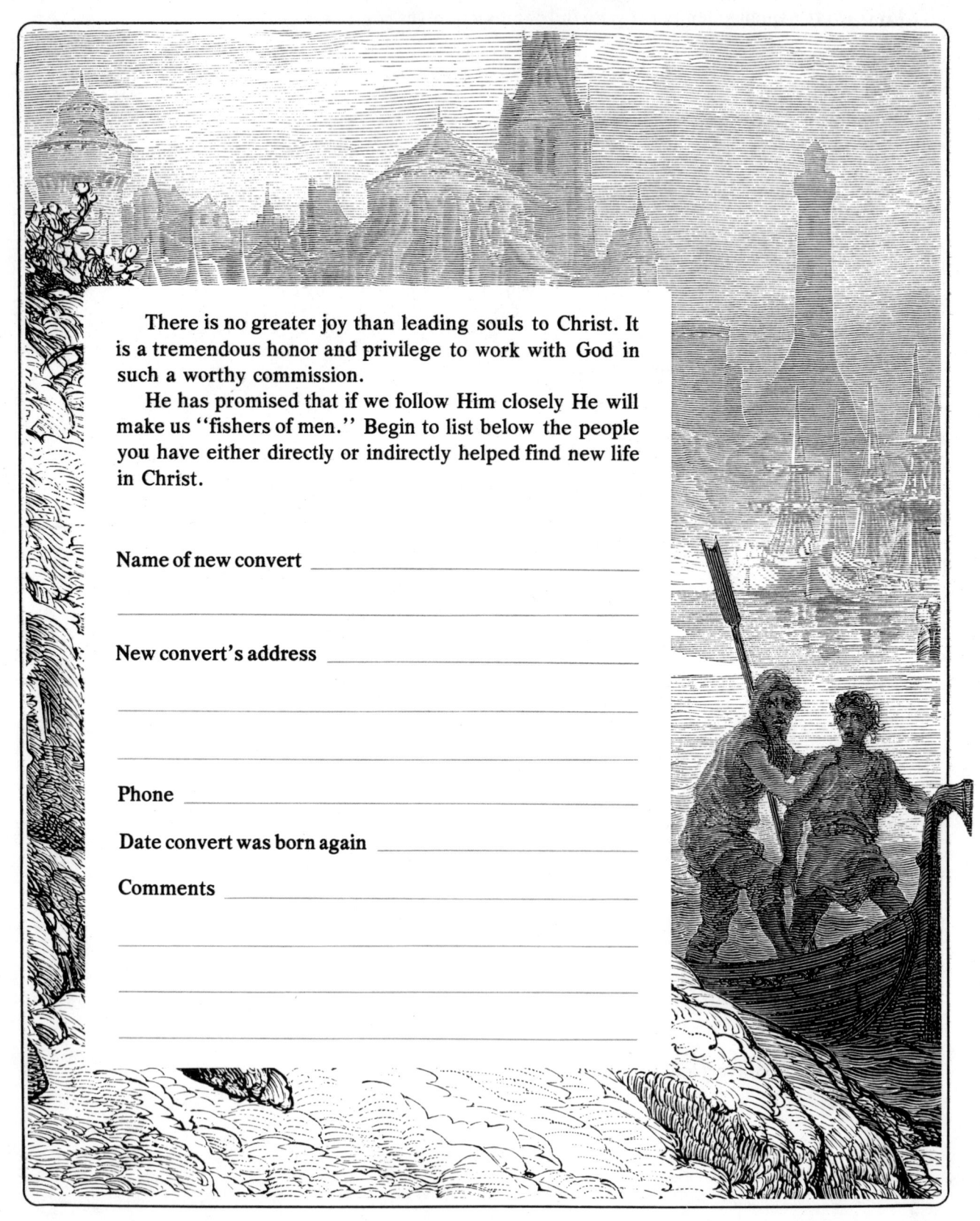

There is no greater joy than leading souls to Christ. It is a tremendous honor and privilege to work with God in such a worthy commission.

He has promised that if we follow Him closely He will make us "fishers of men." Begin to list below the people you have either directly or indirectly helped find new life in Christ.

Name of new convert _____

New convert's address _____

_____

_____

Phone _____

Date convert was born again _____

Comments _____

_____

_____

_____

Name of new convert _____

New convert's address _____

Phone _____

Date convert was born again _____

Comments _____
_____


Name of new convert _____

New convert's address _____

Phone _____

Date convert was born again _____

Comments _____
_____


Name of new convert _____

New convert's address _____

Phone _____

Date convert was born again _____

Comments _____
_____


Name of new convert _____

New convert's address _____

Phone _____

Date convert was born again _____

Comments _____
_____

# Power From God Journal

Results or victories that I have seen come from being filled with the Holy Spirit!

Results!

**Results!**

**Results!**

# CERTIFICATE of GRADUATION

## LIFE IN CHRIST
### A Primary Text and Registry for Christians

This certifies that _____

has completed the course of study prescribed by the above text, and is entitled to this certificate of graduation.

In witness whereof, we affix our signatures at

_____
(location)

on the _____ day of _____ A.D. 19___

_____
Pastor

_____
Discipler

# A Special Thank You

It is very exciting for us to hear the numerous reports from those who have completed this text. We appreciate the time and effort that you have put into it and we hope that it has been a valuable tool to help you grow in your relationship with God.

We would very much like to hear your comments regarding the text and any helpful suggestions you may have for improvement.

Comments: _____
_____
_____
_____
_____
_____
_____
_____
_____
_____

As a special way of saying thank you, we would like to send you a little gift. (book, tape, record, article, etc.)

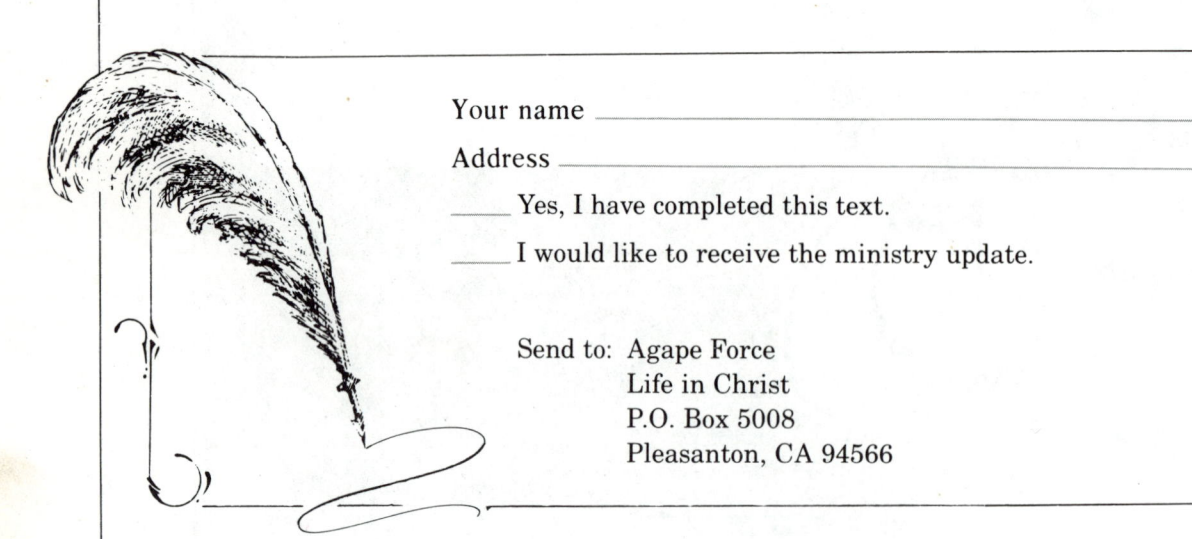

Your name _____
Address _____
____ Yes, I have completed this text.
____ I would like to receive the ministry update.

Send to: Agape Force
Life in Christ
P.O. Box 5008
Pleasanton, CA 94566

(If you do not wish to tear this page out, you have permission to duplicate it, fill out copy and send it in.)